LIVING MEDITATION

*From Principle
to Practice*

C. Alexander Simpkins, Ph.D.
Annellen M. Simpkins, Ph.D.

CHARLES E. TUTTLE CO., INC.
BOSTON ❧ RUTLAND, VERMONT ❧ TOKYO

First published in 1997 by Tuttle Publishing, an imprint of Periplus Editions (HK) Ltd., with editorial offices at 153 Milk Street, Boston, Massachusetts 02109.

Library of Congress Cataloging-in-Publication Data

Simpkins, C. Alexander.
    Living meditation : from principle to practice / by C. Alexander Simpkins, Annellen M. Simpkins.
        p. cm.
    Includes bibliographical references.
    ISBN 0-8048-3114-9
    1. Meditation. 2. Pragmatism. I. Simpkins, Annellen M. II. Title.
BL627.S54 1997
291.4'35—dc21   97-4165
                                                     CIP

Distributed by

USA	Japan	Berkeley Books Pte. Ltd.
Charles E. Tuttle Co., Inc.	Tuttle Shokai Ltd.	5 Little Road #08-01
RR 1 Box 231-5	1-21-13, Seki	Singapore 536983
North Clarendon, VT 05759	Tama-ku, Kawasaki-shi	Tel: (65) 280-3320
Tel: (800) 526-2778	Kanagawa-ken 214, Japan	Fax: (65) 280-6290
Fax: (800) FAX-TUTL	Tel: (044) 833-0225	
	Fax: (044) 822-0413	
	Southeast Asia	

First edition
05 04 03 02 01 00 99 98 97   1 3 5 7 9 10 8 6 4 2
Printed in the United States of America

Book design by Jill Winitzer
Cover art by Carmen Z. Simpkins

Carmen Z. Simpkins' abstract expressionist paintings suggest mood, movement, and mysticism. Simpkins has been painting for 75 years. Her first solo show took place in Camden, Maine, in 1962 at the Broadlawn Gallery. She has exhibited throughout the world, and her works are in private collections in Europe and the Americas. She continues to paint at her studio-gallery in Sebastian, Florida.

For our parents, Carmen and Nat Simpkins
and Naomi and Herbert Minkin,
and our children,
Alura L. Simpkins and C. Alexander Simpkins

Contents

INTRODUCTION

The West is known for having a practical, behavioral orientation to life. We take pride in doing what is efficient and effective. Pragmatism, a philosophy that guides American thought, is concerned with what is useful, what works. In the East, the driving effort has been toward enlightenment, higher knowledge, and spirituality. Yoga, Buddhism, Zen, and Taoism—the wisdom of the East—have all illuminated the dark reaches of the mind through meditation.

Today, with nearly instantaneous global communication, the mysterious philosophies of the East do not seem so foreign to the West. People all around the world are searching for a way in which East and West can work together, for a path to a life that is both successful and spiritually fulfilling.

This book offers useful ways to apply the Eastern wisdom of meditation to improving your life. We caution you to keep in mind that meditation is never simply a limited set of techniques. If you keep meditating, a transformation of attitude takes place that is deeper. Meditation guides you in how to approach problems, how to create your own techniques, how to find the Way and then follow its path. Everyday involvements take on greater personal meaning, becoming opportunities to learn from, as you apply a meditative approach to life.

WHAT IS IN THIS BOOK

Part One presents the philosophical principles underlying meditation. Yoga, Taoism, Buddhism and its later outgrowth of Zen Buddhism offer different perspectives that make the spiritual dimensions of life accessible. American Pragmatism, our indigenous philosophy, adds a rationale for making use of what is effective. Meditation, though rooted in religious and mystical traditions, can also be useful in everyday life, as this book shows.

Part Two takes you step by step through the process of meditation. Developing basic skills with your mind and working in harmony with your body ultimately lead to greater fulfillment of spirit.

Part Three, "Applications," is divided into two sections, "Mental Functioning" and "Healthy Functioning." Each chapter guides you with exercises on how to enhance a certain aspect of your life by applying techniques drawn from the insights of Eastern philosophy.

HOW TO USE THIS BOOK

Meditation is best learned by doing, not just by reading about it. Experiment with the exercises presented throughout the book. Some skills may take time to develop; others may come more rapidly. What comes easily and what is more challenging vary from person to person. Work with your own individuality and be willing to be yourself. Sincerity in practice is the greatest help.

Read each exercise completely through. Then put the book down and try it. We offer many different possibilities in some of the exercises. You are encouraged to make the exercises your own. If one idea fits and another does not, use the appropriate one and do not concern yourself with the other. Trust yourself throughout the process and enjoy.

Krishna and Balarama seated before Brahma
Bhagwan, eighteenth-century India, Panjab Hills, Kulu.
Opaque watercolor and gold on paper, 1794.
Edwin Binney III Collection. San Diego Museum of Art.

PART ONE

Philosophies: Eastern Signposts for Western Trails

Long prior to the age of reflection is the thinking of the mind. Out of darkness it came insensibly into the marvelous light of to-day.

—Ralph Waldo Emerson

The philosophies of the East have had a profound effect on human civilization. Dating back before recorded history, Yoga developed methods of mental and physical discipline that are still studied today. Focused concentration and breath control were the doorways to higher consciousness. Later, the Eastern philosophies of Taoism and Buddhism built upon the foundation of Yoga but developed insights in new directions. Lao-tzu, the first to gather together the Taoist philosophy in a profound little book, the *Tao te Ching*, is considered the originator of Taoist theory. Siddhartha Gautama became known as the Buddha after his enlightenment under the Bodhi tree. He founded the tradition of

Buddhism that lives on in many forms today. Bodhidharma's single-minded devotion to absolute awareness spawned the growth of an entirely new form of Buddhism, Zen. The creative intent of Lao-tzu, Buddha, and Bodhidharma did not end with their own lives but continued to evolve as others set their intellectual and spiritual energies to the further development of these philosophies. Externally these philosophies have changed over the centuries as they were reinterpreted, but the inner message remains unaltered. Important principles are hidden within, filled with timeless wisdom that can improve the quality of your life.

What is useful and leads to effective consequences has been the criterion for people in the West, following scientific philosophy. William James, one of the founding fathers of the American philosophy of Pragmatism, said that Pragmatism always asks, What difference would it make in practice? This question is more important today than ever before. Eastern philosophy offers us a way to find an answer to the mysteries of life.

The great traditions of meditation we discuss will put you in touch with deeper pools of insight from the past. Then, through guidance and exercises, we will show you how to make the best insights of these theories useful additions to your own meditative abilities.

1
YOGA: YOKING THE
MIND TO SEEK TRUTH

Yoga is restraining the mind-stuff from taking various forms. At that time the seer rests in his own (unmodified) state.

—Patanjali

Yoga is an ancient practice that links together many different philosophies. There are Taoist Yogas, Hindu Yogas, Buddhist Yogas, and even Western Yogic methods (such as the spiritual exercises of Saint Ignatius Loyola). Yoga has been applied by many classes of people: nobles and warriors, priests and healers, merchants and laborers. Yoga is ageless and timeless, not limited by just one set of philosophical concepts. What makes Yoga unique is that it is a practical system, not only a philosophy. The result is that you get something out of it: health, self-discipline, and raised consciousness.

Yoga disciplines the mind and body by various combinations of exercises, with concentration and meditation. Practitioners learn how to hold their mind and then direct it at will wherever and to whatever they choose. An expression in Yoga, "To make Samyana," refers to the practice of controlling and directing the mind to accomplish certain goals.

The word *yoga* means "yoke" or "union." The Yogi trains persistently, disciplining mind and body to gain control, yoking mind to body, withdrawing from the illusory world of the senses. By searching inward, the Yogi discovers the true knowledge of reality that links the individual to the universal.

Yogic theory, drawn from Hinduism, holds that people have a soul, or self, called Atman. The goal of Yoga is to connect Atman to Brahman. Atman is like a drop of water, the individual; Braman is like the ocean, the universal. Through enlightened knowledge of your true self, your individual soul becomes one with universal consciousness. The drop of water returns to the sea.

Buddha started as a Yogi. He studied under a famous teacher, Alara, known to be a master of Yoga. Buddha rejected Yogic philosophy but incorporated many of its principles into his new philosophical religion of Buddhism. Much of Buddhist meditation and codes of conduct derives from Yoga.

Patanjali, in the second century B.C., codified the ancient systems of Yoga. He was careful to point out that he had not created these systems but rather was gathering and organizing wisdom that had existed for centuries.

Patanjali clarified how Yoga helps practitioners reach a higher consciousness. The first step is to change your mental attitude, to live morally according to rules of conduct, striving not to engage in harmful actions, such as stealing or harming others. The Yogi also takes on good bodily habits: careful diet and body purification. The modern health-food movement is based in part on the early Yogic diet, which included fresh fruits, vegetables, and grains.

The Yogi then learns control of the breath. *Prana* is universal vital energy. Breath control is key to taking in and directing the energy of prana for health, vitality, and higher consciousness. Focused concentration, learning to empty the mind of thoughts and to keep it still, also develops mental proficiency. Restraint through exercising the will is one of the central principles employed in Yoga. Withdrawing from worldly concerns reveals the deeper essence of reality.

Yogis focus on three planes of meditation: first, the body; second, the mind and intellectual world; and finally, the Absolute. In Yoga meditation, the Yogi becomes a part of the total field of concentration, just as a mirror that reflects the color blue, appears blue. Through the discipline of meditation, Yogis acquire health, longevity, and even extraordinary powers, but these benefits are considered secondary. The highest aim of Yoga is enlightenment.

There are many ways to achieve enlightenment through different types of Yoga. Each has developed into its own form, with its own methods and philosophy. Hatha Yoga, widely practiced in the West, takes the path of body postures combined with breath control and concentration. In Raja Yoga, higher consciousness is sought through directly training the mind with the will. Clearing the mind with meditation exercises allows the true source of deeper wisdom to emerge from within. Bhakti Yoga, the way of love, practices charitable, self-sacrificing, religious devotion. Personal limitations are transcended as the individual finds union with God. Karma Yoga, the way of work, teaches ethics and values. Work offers salvation through service and fulfillment of one's destiny. Mantra Yoga uses chanting to help focus the mind and energy. Chanting "Om," Sanskrit for "Oneness," is the way to gain knowledge and destroy obstacles, according to Patanjali. Gnani Yoga uses philosophical concepts to transcend mundane consciousness through logic. Practitioners study philosophy and then meditate on the insights, transcending self to become part of the "Allness." By means of these and other methods, Yogis seek to unite with the greater whole, the true self.

*It is light inside, light outside, a light along and holier
than holy. It is the light that lights all light, uncaused.
And it is the light of the self.*

—The Upanishads

Buddha-to-be-Sakyamuni.
India, Bihar, probably Bodhgaya,
late tenth century, Pala period granite.
Gift of the Asian Arts Committee.
San Diego Museum of Art.

2
BUDDHISM: TRUTH IS WITHIN THE MIND

*Your mind has its own mysterious nature of
brightness and purity.*

—Buddha, in the Surangama Sutra

The original enlightenment of Siddhartha Gautama (560–480 B.C.), as he was sitting in meditation under the Bodhi (fig) tree, became the foundation for a philosophy that has swept across the globe to become one of the world's great religions.

Siddhartha gave up the luxuries of his high station in life to search for the answers to human suffering and understand the true meaning of life. He joined the ascetics who lived in the forest, depriving himself of bodily comforts. By severing himself from all attachments in this material world, he hoped to find salvation in the spiritual world. Close to death from starvation, he was struck with the realization that despite his years of sincere effort, he was no closer to any insight. Consequently, he took food and water to bring himself back to health. That night, with renewed strength, he sat under a Bodhi tree in meditation. As the dawn's light peeked over the horizon,

Siddhartha was awakened and filled with inner happiness and peace. He knew the answer to the problems of life. He was called to share this knowledge with the world.

BUDDHA'S MESSAGE

Buddha's message is simple and consistent: Follow the middle way. Neither extreme, worldly pleasures nor ascetic denial makes you happy. The way of moderation is the true path to follow. Buddha expressed his teachings as Four Noble Truths. First, we must recognize that suffering and frustration are part of life. We suffer from pain, sickness, and inevitable death. Second is that this suffering comes from clinging, craving, and grasping; the world seems to offer many comforts and pleasures, but these are not satisfying. The third truth reveals that the cause of suffering can be eliminated by giving up craving. Finally, the way to let go of craving is by following the Eightfold Path: right views, right aspirations, right speech, right behavior, right livelihood, right effort, right thoughts, and right contemplation. The first two involve coming to an understanding of the human condition. The next four teach us how to abandon worldly entanglements. The final two help us develop skills in meditation, the inner mental practice of Buddha's Way.

THE EVOLUTION OF BUDDHISM

Buddhism formally split into two main branches: Mahayana and Hinayana, later named Theravada. The Theravadins remained true to the original teachings of Buddha. This branch holds that each person, *arhat*, follows the Eightfold Path through secluded contemplation in a monastery to find nirvana (enlightenment). To be an arhat, a saint, reaching nirvana individually, is the Theravadins' idea of perfection. Simple, austere, and traditional, this form of Buddhism has flourished most strongly in Southeast Asia.

Mahayana is the more innovative form; by adding a multitude of variations, sects, and Buddhas, it has made Buddhism a religion for the masses throughout the world. The Mahayana ideal, the *bodhisattva*, lives differently from the Theravadin arhant, who retires from everyday life to quietly rest at peace in nirvana. Once enlightened, the bodhisattva turns away from nirvana and returns to the world to enlighten others. Not until all are free from suffering can the bodhisattva be free as well. We are all one; therefore, no one may be excluded—all must be enlightened equally. Salvation for all means that all are held sacred. The modern interpretation leads many Buddhists to involve themselves with peace movements, environmentalism, and many kinds of benevolent action.

THE IMPORTANCE OF MEDITATION

Like Socrates of ancient Greece, Buddhism values wisdom as the highest good.

> *The greatest fault to be avoided is Ignorance. To overcome the enemy Ignorance, one Requireth Wisdom. The best method of acquiring Wisdom is unfaltering endeavor (in Yogically directed meditation). (Evans-Wentz 1935, 65)*

Buddhism emphasizes meditation as the only effective pathway to wisdom. Many of the sutras teach people how to meditate. The Diamond Sutra, the inspiration for Hui-neng's enlightenment, gives this instruction for meditation: "The mind should be kept independent of any thoughts that arise within it" (Price and Mou-lam 1990, 33). Truth is within the mind, detached from the problems of everyday life and even detached from the self. Buddha rejected having a concept of self. Self is empty; truth is empty—beyond good and evil, beyond all duality, and even beyond concepts or words. As Buddha said, "Truth is undeclarable." This truth is called buddhahood.

Buddhism confounds logic further by explaining that attaining buddhahood is not really attaining anything. Buddhahood is nonattainment, release. Everyone already has the capacity within to achieve nirvana, but few come to realize it. Wisdom is accessible to all who sincerely turn attention inward and meditate.

BUDDHIST SUTRAS

Buddhists also believe that wisdom can be achieved by reading and studying sutras. Sutras are ancient writings, originally attributed to Buddha, that were compiled over the centuries following his death. Many different sects of Buddhism have been inspired by the message of particular sutras. Sutras push the limits of intellectual thought in addition to providing spiritual inspiration.

The Diamond Sutra, written about A.D. 350, is one of the oldest books still in existence. The original sixteen-foot scroll can be seen at the British Museum in London. In this sutra, a part of the larger Wisdom Sutras, Buddha answers questions asked by Subhuti, one of his disciples. Buddha explains that seekers of the Way must give up their usual modes of thinking and experiencing. The answer requires a different kind of thinking than logic and reason. To help people discover this state of mind, the sutra presents a paradox: "It neither is nor is not" (Price and Mou-lam 1990, 24). The seeker may use reason along the way, but eventually it must be discarded. Reason is like a boat, a raft to cross the river. It is useful to get you across, but once you reach the other shore, it should be discarded.

The Heart Sutra, another work from the Wisdom Sutras, is a short work that persuasively describes the true nature of reality as Buddhism views it: "Form is emptiness and emptiness is form." The enlightened person knows that all things are impermanent and in this way empty. Yet our senses tell us that there is much to experience; form seems very real. With Buddhist insight, people can experience the relative reality of things in this world and yet realize that ultimately nothing is real. This sutra is chanted daily in many Zen temples as a mental corrective for clearing the mind.

The Avatamsaka Sutra is a large collection of works, spanning the first to fourth centuries. This sutra is based on another important principle in Buddhism, that all objects are interrelated and interpenetrate one another. The universal is reflected in the individual, and the individual is reflected in the universal. All is contained in the one, and the one is in all.

Monks Crossing Bridge.
Nagasawa Rosetsu, Japanese 1754–99, Edo period.
Ink and color on paper, n.d.
Gift of Mrs. Leon D. Bonnet. San Diego Museum of Art.

3

ZEN BUDDHISM: EVERYDAY LIFE IS TRULY ENLIGHTENING

If a reader is brave enough and goes straight forward in his meditation, no delusions can disturb him. He will become enlightened just as did the patriarchs in India and in China, probably even better.

—Paul Reps

EARLY ZEN IN CHINA

Bodhidharma (440–528), the founder of Zen, began a tradition that has grown to become a worldwide phenomenon. He gave Zen a foundation in a pure and simple approach to living with complete awareness of our original nature. Bodhidharma learned Buddhism in India and excelled in his studies. After his teacher died, he traveled to China to bring the teachings to a new land. It is said that when Bodhidharma arrived in China, Zen was born.

Bodhidharma believed that the mind's capacity is limitless. He pointed out in one of his lectures that

Buddha is Sanskrit for what you call aware, miraculously aware. Responding, perceiving, arching your brows, blinking your eyes, moving your hands and feet, it is all your miraculously aware nature. And this nature is the mind. (Pine 1989, 25)

He believed that through this intense awareness, people would live according to their true nature. Bodhidharma's own life exemplified his teachings. His absolute commitment to Zen was shown when he sat in meditation facing a cave wall for nine years. This intense devotion was a testament to living meditation!

Bodhidharma's teachings were passed along from teacher to student for a number of generations. The consistent message was to be awake and aware. As the Fourth Patriarch Tao-hsin said, "The mind is awake and never ceasing; the awakened mind is always present" (Dumoulin 1988, 100). Zen taught people to use meditation to wake up. Nothing else mattered.

The Sixth Patriarch, Hui-neng (638–713), believed that the awake and aware state of Zen could happen in a sudden flash of insight. Anyone could experience it, no matter what his or her background or education. His own enlightenment occurred while he was selling firewood in the marketplace. As he listened to a man reciting the Diamond Sutra, he was so moved by the words that he suddenly became enlightened.

ZEN MIND: EVERYDAY MIND

Zen teaches that enlightened awareness does not come from somewhere beyond. The kingdom of Buddha is in this world now, nowhere else. It comes as part of everyday life, being fully present in the immediate moment. By meditating during daily activities, even the most mundane, the Zen Buddhist maintains an enlightened state while remaining in this world. Zen monasteries incorporate a daily regimen that always includes working in addition to meditation. Zen awareness should continue through the entire day.

Zen monastic life follows a strict moral code. Each monk vows to abide by the required moral standards: no killing, stealing, sex, lying, or alcohol. They follow routines each day—early morning meditation, meals, work, more meditation, and sleep—that help them maintain these precepts. The strict disciplined life in the monastery keeps the monks on track.

As all become more adept in Zen practice, they can perform their everyday routines in a natural, effortless manner. The link between thought and action becomes spontaneous and direct. "In walking just walk. In sitting just sit. Above all, don't wobble" (Watts 1957, 135).

Without using words, Zen masters often taught pupils to experience the Zen state of mind. Lin-chi (d. 866) became famous for bringing his students to instant enlightenment. He was also the founder of one of the two main sects of Zen still practiced today, Rinzai Zen. This story is a typical encounter. A monk asked, "What is the meaning of Buddhism?" Lin-chi held his stick straight up. The monk shouted. Then Lin-chi struck him. Lin-chi helped his student return to being fully present, not speculating abstractly. The strike is startling. There is no time for thought, only an immediate experience. Zen encourages you to respond without thought to all of life's situations. You reflexively try to jump out of the way if you stray into the path of a car. Similarly, in the awakened state, you simply are there, reacting to what happens, and you respond. Japanese Zen monk Bankei (1622–1693) called this way of being "the unborn mind."

> *The unborn mind of the Buddhas that all people*
> *receive from their parents when they're born is*
> *wonderfully bright and illuminating. No one—that*
> *includes all of you—is ever separated from it.*
> *(Waddell 1984, 66)*

JAPANESE ZEN

Zen was brought from China to Japan sometime around the twelfth century. The early Japanese Zen monk Dogen (1200–1253) was considered one of the greatest Zen monks of all time. His devotion to Zen—and only Zen—reminds us of Bodhidharma. He gave up all worldly possessions and pursued meditation single-mindedly. He formally introduced the practice of *zazen*, meditative sitting. He believed that by our sitting regularly in disciplined meditation, all problems could be solved. The exact instructions are given in Part Two "Meditation Basics: The ABCs of Meditation." Through zazen the mind becomes clear, and there is unity between mind and body. Dogen said, "Therefore, if you cast aside completely the thoughts and concepts of the mind and concentrate on zazen alone, you attain to an intimacy with the Way. The attainment of the Way is truly accomplished with the body. For this reason I urge you to concentrate on zazen" (Dumoulin 1990, 78). Dogen's teachings became the foundation for Soto Zen, one of the major worldwide sects of Zen today.

Zen evolved as the Japanese brought direct Zen experience into the realm of action. Zen masters expressed their Zen enlightenment in archery, poetry, calligraphy, martial arts, flower arranging, and the tea ceremony. In all the Zen arts, as they have been called, the external product is secondary to the inner attitude.

> *To the degree that the pupil can summon up*
> *courage for the necessary self-discipline and this*
> *keeps pace with his artistic ability, he will find, not*
> *only as an artist but also as a human being, a spe-*
> *cial relationship to his performance, to this quiet,*
> *unswerving creation out of inner harmony.*
> *(Herrigel 1958, 23)*

Hakuin (1685–1768), one of the most dynamic, prolific, and influential Rinzai monks in Japan, developed a unique style of painting and calligraphy that was "stamped with his own immediate experience" (Dumoulin 1990, 489). He also codified *koans* as a way to teach Zen. To Hakuin, koans were central for learning Zen. The famous koan "What is the sound of one hand clapping?" was created by Hakuin to help students begin the process. He organized the koans into categories that permitted a hierarchical curriculum for teaching the Rinzai approach. Each level was to be mastered before moving on to the next. Throughout his life Hakuin proselytized the power of meditation and koans.

The koan offers a puzzling question that does not have a rational answer. Only when students enter into enlightened awareness will they be able to give an acceptable response. Because rational thought does not help, students are forced to turn away from everything they ever learned. The koan, if taken seriously, inevitably leads to a great doubt that takes precedence over all else. Hakuin said, "At the bottom of great doubt lies great awakening. If you doubt fully you will awaken fully" (Dumoulin 1990, 381). The koan helps focus attention and facilitates the discovery of transcendental insight, which leads to enlightenment.

CONCLUSION

Zen offers an experiential path to wisdom. The main vehicle is meditation, applied through koans, arts, sitting or moving, work or play, eating and sleeping. No matter what you do or where you are, you can always be practicing Zen.

Ho Hsien-ku (with Lotus Flowers)
(from the *Eight Immortal Taoists*).
Chinese, c. 1900, Ivory.
Gift of the James P. Whiterow Family.
San Diego Museum of Art.

4
TAOISM: TRUTH IS A
WAY OF LIFE

Tao is unfathomable fullness
As night is part of day
The concept points beyond itself
And in its going stays

—C. Alexander Simpkins

Taoism is an ancient philosophy that originated in China before recorded history. Lao-tzu is credited with being the first to express Taoism in writing. He lived during the fifth century B.C., a time of political and social turbulence in China. His Taoist teachings showed people a way to stop fighting the problems of the day and instead take the path of noninterference, to let nature take its course. Before he left China on a trackless journey, he told the gatekeeper at the city limits all about Tao. This became the metaphorical book entitled the *Tao te Ching*, which still speaks to us today.

Lao-tzu's inspirational influence was carried forward by the teachings of Chuang-tzu (399–295 B.C.). The style of Chuang-tzu's books on Taoism is very different from the *Tao te Ching*, yet the philosophical principles are consistent. He presents Taoism through anecdotes, narratives, and satire. Chuang-tzu was well versed in the literature and philosophies of his time. He liked best to articulate Taoism through imaginary dialogues with the leaders of other philosophies, such as Confucius. Chuang-tzu's works on Taoism, *The Texts of Taoism*, along with the *Tao te Ching*, leave a legacy that inspires us to look deeper, to discover that we have a place in the nature of all things, the Tao.

THE TAO

Taoism is based in the Tao itself, the inner nature of all things, the Way. Like the Buddhist concept of enlightenment, it is beyond words.

> *The Tao that can be told of*
> *Is not the Absolute Tao*
> *The Names that can be given*
> *Are not Absolute Names*
> —*Tao te Ching*, chapter 1, translated by Lin Yutang

Tao is beyond expression in words and thoughts. The source of all concepts, prior to concepts, Tao cannot be defined. When you try to use a concept to define Tao, you lose the Tao because it does not fit into a conceptual box. Tao is limitless, unbounded, unnameable. The Tao is a way you follow, a path, not something you can think about or conceptualize. To become one with the Tao is to be one with the inner nature of all things, ever changing and evolving, never static. As you can imagine, Tao can be quite mysterious. Not only is the Tao mystical; it can also be useful.

Tao is all pervading
And its use is inexhaustible
　　　　　—*Tao te Ching*, chapter 4, translated by Lin Yutang

Taoism offers both a spiritual feeling about life along with practical advice for living intuitively, using Tao as a guide.

Chuang-tzu wrote, "Hear not with your ears, but with your mind; not with your mind, but with your spirit" (Yutang 1952, 647). When we act based on this intuition of the spirit, our actions are correct, through our Oneness with the Tao.

YIN AND YANG

Yin-yang theory is older than Taoism and permeates Chinese thought. Its doctrine is simple, yet its influence is profound. Lao-tzu and Chuang-tzu characterized much of their theories through this doctrine, making it an important part of Taoism. Almost everyone has seen the yin-yang symbol: a circle, half black and half white, with a dot of white on the black and vice versa. Yin symbolizes the passive, receptive, weak, and destructive. Yang is positive, active, strong, and constructive. Within the whole, there are always the opposites. The yin-yang symbol illustrates that even within the black there is some white, and in the white there must be some black. Opposites are in a dynamic balance, always in relation to each other. Eastern medicine, for example, analyzes the workings of body and spirit in terms of yin and yang. Illness occurs when yin and yang are out of balance. Treatment restores balance. Dryness is moistened, heat or inflamation is cooled, overstraining is balanced by rest. Once back in tune with central harmony, yin and yang dissolve into the Oneness of Tao.

NONACTION

A central premise of Taoism is the idea that nonaction is the pathway to success. Many problems in the world arise from too much effort, too much contending and pushing against others. According to Taoism, noninterference in events is often the best action to take. Let the stream of events flow in their natural course, with the river of life itself. Do not fight your way upstream against the current. Instead, get in tune, swim with the current; you will soon be able to maneuver and proceed without effort, comfortably sped along by the currents of the Way.

> *The mind of the perfect man is like a mirror. It does*
> *not lean forward or backward in its response to*
> *things. (Chan 1963, 207)*

Taoism advises people to be receptive. Emptying the mind of trivial and unnecessary data allows it to be responsive and open. Taoists value emptiness. The usefulness of a cup is in its emptiness.

Taoists seek the balanced, quiet stillness at the center, emptiness. There, at the center point—before concepts, beyond differentiation into the dynamic opposites of yin and yang—is found the original principle, which applies to all things:

> *"One who knows Tao will surely penetrate the prin-*
> *ciple of things," said the spirit of the North Sea,*
> *"and one who penetrates the principle of things will*
> *surely understand their application in various situ-*
> *ations." (Chan 1962, 207)*

5

PRAGMATISM: TRUTH IS ACTION'S INSTRUMENT

*Pragmatism unstiffens all our theories, limbers
them up and sets each one at work. Being nothing
essentially new, it harmonizes with many ancient
philosophic tendencies.*

—William James

The word *pragmatism* derives from the Greek word *pragma,*
meaning "action," from which our words *practice* and *practical* derive. Charles Pierce first introduced the idea of
Pragmatism in an article, "How to Make Our Ideas Clear," published
in *Popular Science Monthly* in 1879. Pierce stated that beliefs are really
rules for action. Meaning is merely the behavior that action produces.

William James developed a branch of Pragmatism that is especially relevant for meditation. He believed that philosophy leads to
action because thought and action are linked. The best test was, Is it
useful? Can it be of service? Not, Is it a profound ultimate reality? The
Pragmatists did not accept truth that does not do something.

James questioned not only whether something was useful but
whether it could become an instrument of action and thus be verified by
action. Actions are the grounds to test truths, to make them work for us.

We do not verify everything we know and use, nor should we. We use many temporary constructions, workable situations. For example, we do not need to understand everything about the theory of electricity to turn on a light switch. We just need to know how to do it. When we need light, flipping the switch is enough.

Truths are in process, since action is a process. James pointed out that there may not be one final truth but rather many truthful ways of adapting to reality. Verification need not be absolute or timeless. We have come to accept the idea that what we know now as true may not be so for all time: Truth in 1896 may not be truth for 1996 or 2096. New countries now exist; Russia is no longer the USSR; Germany is one country, not two. Advances in technology have shown us that what was impossible a few years ago is quite possible today. For example, computer memory has increased geometrically over the past few years. Many may vividly remember just a short time ago how amazed we were by the astounding new capabilities of our very first 28K computer. Now gigabytes are the norm, and the old Commodores, Ataris, and Apple IIe's gather dust. New forms of data storage have made it possible to store and process information formerly never correlated, leading to new discoveries from the compounding of ideas. Medical discoveries now cure diseases that formerly led to inevitable death. And yet, amid all this modern progress, wisdom from ancient Eastern philosophy, unknown to the West for centuries, is now accepted as having many important truths. The future approaches, and we wonder at how rapidly things change.

We need a way of comprehending life that somehow takes account of this ever changing reality but does not leave us adrift, lost at sea in vague relativism, with no compass with which to find our way. We can navigate the ocean of reality without permanent land masses by using temporary constructions of thought, maps for action to follow. Even though these maps might not be the actual territory, they correspond to it for now and can be useful.

Some philosophies are optimistic. Others are pessimistic. James hoped that Pragmatism would be "melioristic," always seeking to improve things. By adopting Pragmatism's orientation to meditation, you do not have to choose one position or the other as the ultimate truth. Our way of meditation, drawn from the classics of Eastern thought, can help you to *live* meditation. Whether you know a lot about Eastern philosophy, whether you are a beginner or well on the path, meditation can be useful. That is what living meditation is all about!

PART TWO
Meditation Basics: The ABCs of Meditation

🌿

If you never wholly give yourself up to the chair you sit in, but always keep your leg-and-body-muscles half contracted for a rise; if you breathe eighteen or nineteen instead of sixteen times a minute, and never quite breathe out at that—what mental mood can you be in but one of inner panting and expectancy, and how can the future and its worries possibly forsake your mind? On the other hand, how can they gain admission to your mind if your brow be unruffled, your respiration calm and complete, and your muscles all relaxed?

—William James

Meditation is first of all an experience. The more you do it, the more natural it becomes. In this section we present the basics of meditation. Later we offer ways to use and adapt meditation to many practical areas of life. All these applications are drawn from the meditative skills included in this chapter. Other applications are also possible, and the various techniques may be substituted for a particular application. By practicing these meditations regularly, you share in a tradition that has enriched the lives of people around the world for centuries.

Some traditions, such as Zen and classical Buddhism, instruct practitioners to empty their mind. Other approaches, like Gnani Yoga, teach people to fill their mind with universal truths of wisdom. Both emptying and filling can be accomplished by using your attention in specific ways. We show you how to fix your attention or allow it to float freely, attending to nothing. Finally, there is the middle way that is neither one way nor the other, the balance point between opposites. Through meditation we seek to find this harmony, the Oneness beyond name and concept.

6

GETTING
READY

The gate to enlightenment lies before us,
Though we hesitate at the door
Let us draw up a comfortable cushion
And rest it on the floor.

—C. Alexander Simpkins

MEDITATION POSTURES

Fundamental, simple postures are most conducive to meditation: sitting, standing, and lying down. Once you can meditate comfortably, you can extend the meditative mind into more aspects of your daily life, such as when you are moving and doing things.

Some people find it difficult to sit in the meditative posture. The following exercise helps you discover this posture and become at ease with it.

FINDING YOUR SITTING POSTURE

The sitting position is the most common meditative posture. Sit cross-legged on the floor or on a small cushion. Close your eyes fully or partially. Keep your back straight and your shoulders open without hunching forward, so that your breathing passages are clear and your head is straight.

You may place your hands in any one of the standard meditative positions. Extend your arms so that the backs of your hands are over your knees. Clasp your forefinger and thumb in a circle, with the other three fingers extended. Another method is to fold your two hands together. Fingertips can be either together or with a rounded space between them. A third method is to place your hands one on top of the other, palms up, with thumbs touching. Find the position that is most comfortable for you.

Sway forward very slightly, then back. Rock forward, then back, several times—not so far as to lose your balance, just enough to feel a gentle shift. Feel the motion as you move; experience how you pass through a natural balance point at the center, and then go beyond on each side. Gently rock back to that center point and remain there for a moment. Next, rock sideways: left, then right. Repeat several times, noticing once again as you pass through the center point. Return to the center. When you have found your center, you will feel poised and relaxed, at one with gravity, sitting more effortlessly than usual.

A PLACE TO MEDITATE

People often ask, Where should I meditate? The atmosphere of the place you choose can be very helpful, although once you are well acquainted with meditation, you can do it almost anywhere.

At first, find a quiet place to meditate. It may be a quiet room or even a certain corner in your house. Set up the area with a meditation pillow for sitting and a mat to lie down on. Lighting should be subdued, not too dark or too bright. Some people also like to burn incense or bring in a fragrant or lush plant. Keep it simple, but give it atmosphere. Zen tea rooms are traditionally decorated naturally and simply to create an atmosphere of sanctuary. A single flower in a vase and a lone calligraphic scroll hanging on a blank wall are usually the only decorations. Pillows on a wooden floor make up the furnishings: quiet surroundings to foster a quiet mind.

Here is a meditation room at the Providence Zen Center in Providence, Rhode Island. Notice the two types of pillows, round and square, that can be used for comfortable sitting.

Nature can be inspirational for meditation. Meditation done out-doors, at a park, in the woods, or perhaps in a beautiful garden can help to bring about a feeling of Oneness. Water can also have a calming effect. The beach, the shore of a lake, the edge of a pond, or the banks of a stream can all be possible sites for a meditation session. Some of the meditations included in this book are best done out-doors.

Often people choose to meditate with a group. Sometimes the commitment and momentum of many people embarking on meditation together, striving for enlightenment, can carry you along. Others prefer solitude and privacy, feeling that the group atmosphere is distracting. Whether you choose to meditate with others or alone is a matter of personal preference. There are many meditation centers and retreats springing up all around the world. They offer from hour-long up to month-long retreats for regular meditation. Yet your own personal, private experience, alone or with someone, may be complete. There are no prerequisite conditions, but one: meditate!

Meditation can even be done in the middle of a busy downtown area. In Tokyo, "meditation cafes" offer popular places to go for quiet moments. Speaking is not allowed; even when ordering, customers just point to the items on the menu. All the tables and high-backed chairs face the same direction, so that each customer can enjoy privacy. Patrons relax and calm their mind, while savoring a delicious cup of tea or coffee (Wachter 1994).

The most important consideration in choosing a place to meditate is that you feel at ease there. Return to the same place each time for meditation. Habit and consistency help. Eventually you will find that meditation's blessings flow very naturally in your special meditation place.

A TIME TO MEDITATE

Whenever we have given a lecture on meditation, people complain that their lives are too hectic and busy already and that they could not imagine finding any time to meditate. They are always surprised to discover that meditation can be done in as short a period as one minute and still bring positive effects! How much time you devote to meditation is a very personal matter. Undoubtedly there are wasted moments in your day or evening that you can make use of. A beginner can start off with one or two minutes a day and work up to a half hour, but even ten minutes a day can be effective. The unconscious, inner mind does not function on clock time the way our conscious mind does. Sometimes the deepest meditative experience occurs in a flash. Then again, an insight may evolve over many months of meditative practice.

Meditate at least one time nearly every day. If you are working on something, as described in subsequent chapters, you should meditate several times during the day. Start from where you are, devoting whatever time that you can comfortably fit within your schedule. But above all, meditate regularly! Be faithful to your practice.

7
MEDITATIONS

Meditation's calm
The sweet incense it brings
Restores us to peaceful
Inner wellsprings
Helps us shed all cares
Cools and soothes the soul
Clears the mind
Makes us whole.

—C. Alexander Simpkins

T his section presents exercises for developing basic meditative skills to empty your mind and fill it, strengthen your mind-body link, and learn to work with your unconscious. Practice these exercises so that you are comfortable doing them. In Part Three, "Applications," you will learn how to apply these meditations in practical ways.

EMPTY THE MIND

How turbid, like muddy water!
What may allay the muddiness? Through stillness it
will gradually become clear.
—*Tao te Ching*, chapter 14, translated by J. J. L. Duyvendak

Everyday mind can fill like a muddy pond, stirred up by thoughts, plans, and worries. Emptiness is the pathway that many forms of meditation take to reduce distractions. Clear mind, also referred to as the Buddha mind, is the cornerstone of Zen. Beyond words, clear mind is a limitless perspective, the meditative perspective. This is the foundation for inner work.

By experimenting with these exercises, you will discover a newfound sense of yourself, centered in your intuition.

CLEARING THE WATER MEDITATION

This exercise helps you "warm up" before clearing your mind of distracting thoughts. Sit quietly with your eyes closed. Imagine that you are sitting on the shore of a pond. The pond is alive with activity. Frogs croak; crickets sing; birds fly overhead; a fish jumps out of the water, feeding on insects, splashes back down, and jumps again after a bit, in another spot. Wind whips over the water, stirring up the muddy bottom. All is movement. Then gradually as the day passes, the conditions begin to shift. The wind dies down. The frogs settle in for a nap, the crickets are silent, birds perch in the trees, the fish stops jumping and waits. The pond is quiet. The murky rippled surface calms as the mud sinks to the bottom, and the water is again crystal clear, reflecting the natural surroundings. All is stillness. Imagine this scene vividly. Stay with the quiet, crystal clear water.

MIRROR MIND MEDITATION

When the perfect man employs his mind, it is a mirror. It conducts nothing and anticipates nothing. . . . Thus he is able to deal successfully with all things, and injures none. (Legge, vol. 1 1962, 266)

Clear mind is like a mirror: always empty, yet reflecting the world all around.

Sit upright on the floor, legs crossed, hands resting on your lap. Close your eyes. Vividly visualize your mind as a mirror, clear and empty. Keep this image of a mirror reflecting nothing. If a thought occurs to you, see it as a reflection in the mirror, knowing it is not the mirror, only the reflection. Let the mirror clear again. Eventually fewer reflections appear, until your mirror mind remains clear.

Meditation—relaxed, calm, and one with nature.

CLASSIC ZAZEN

Zazen, sitting meditation, is the classic exercise used in Zen Buddhism. Zen monks spend many hours meditating in this way, seeking to bring about an enlightened state of consciousness that continues to develop. Follow the instructions carefully, and with time and practice you will experience a special calm and quiet awareness that comes from somewhere unknown, within you.

Sit upright, cross-legged, with your hands palms up and the back of each hand resting on each thigh. Let your body be upright and straight—but not rigid—without leaning either left or right. Your head should be held straight, with your ears and shoulders parallel to each other. Hold your tongue loosely against your palate and keep your lips closed and teeth together. Eyes should be closed or half open. Refer back to the exercise on finding your sitting posture (page 30).

Breathe calmly and regularly. As you begin to meditate, clear your mind of all thought. When a thought does arise, notice it and then dismiss it, returning to your calm, clear mind. By continuing to do this over time, you will eventually find that thoughts intrude less and less and that your concentration becomes natural and profound.

FILLING THE MIND TO EMPTY THE MIND

Some forms of meditation fill the mind, perhaps with a visualization, a sound, a chant, or an experience. Filling the mind can help you find your center, calm and alert. As you become focused, your attention will not be easily led off track by distractions. These exercises develop the skills needed to meditate on an image, a sound, or an experience. This form of meditation will be very helpful in the applications described later.

VISUALIZE AN IMAGE

Make a square of your favorite color out of paper. Hang it on a white wall and look at it for a while. Think carefully about your color, experience it deeply. After looking at it for several minutes, close your eyes. An image of the shape in a different color will appear before your eyes.

Later, close your eyes and think of your favorite color. Imagine how it looked on the paper hanging on the wall. Picture it vividly, letting it fill your mind completely. Think of nothing else. Once you have pictured your color for several minutes, imagine that it becomes smaller and smaller, until it shrinks down to a single concentrated dot. Then let it become larger and larger again. Practice this meditation regularly until you can picture your color at will.

VISUALIZE SOUND

You can do a similar meditation with music. Play one of your favorite songs or pieces of music on a tape or CD, preferably quiet, peaceful music without excessive lyrics. Listen to it several times in a row. Pay close attention to all the details of the melody, the instruments, the rhythms. Next, turn off the music and close your eyes. Imagine that you can hear it playing in your mind. Stay with it, thinking of nothing else. Enjoy the music and the meditative experience that accompanies it. Also try it with your eyes open. As you gain in skill, you will learn not to be distracted by external conditions.

MEMORY

It is possible to have a vivid memory that so completely fills your mind that you feel as if you are actually there. To train this ability, go to a place that you like. Perhaps it is the ocean, the woods, a friend's house, a church, a museum—anywhere that you enjoy. Take a moment when you are there to note as many of the details as you can. Look around you. Notice the smells, sounds, how you feel. If possible, close your eyes and vividly imagine the place. Picture it, experience everything about it. Take notes if you like or describe it into a tape recorder. Another possibility is to take pictures so that you capture a visual image of the details.

Later, when you are at home in your meditation place, close your eyes again and remember the place. Re-create the entire experience: sights, sounds, smells, feelings. Experience it fully. Your mind fills with the experience. After you are finished, do you continue to feel at ease and relaxed?

FORGING THE MIND-BODY LINK

For centuries, philosophers have recognized the importance of meditative breathing. Breathing not only keeps us alive but also links the internal energy systems of our body with the outer environment. Every breath, in and out, is part of our harmony with the universe.

As a direct pathway to the link between mind and body, breathing meditations can enhance your harmony. You can focus on your breathing as a way to train your mind to stay focused.

THE COMPLETE BREATH

The complete breath helps free the breathing passages, giving the maximum benefit from a minimum expenditure of energy. It is not forced but rather is a return to full, natural breathing. Infants breathe this way. We can all reclaim our natural birthright, to be supple and relaxed.

COMPLETE BREATH EXERCISE

Stand comfortably, but as straight as possible without straining. Turn your attention inward to your breathing. Breathe in steadily through your nose. Allow the air to fill the upper section of your lungs by letting your diaphragm expand. Let the air move down into the middle part of your lungs, pushing out the lower ribs and chest. Draw the air all the way down into the lower part of your abdomen, allowing it to expand. Do so in one smooth inhalation, permitting your chest cavity to expand in all directions. Retain the breath for a few seconds. Then exhale very slowly, beginning from the abdomen. Draw your abdomen in gently, lifting it slightly as the air leaves your lungs. Keep your attention focused on your body as the air flows in and out.

You might find it easier to experience your breathing more fully by placing your hands lightly over your abdomen. You should feel an in-and-out movement in your abdomen as the air enters and leaves. You do not need to take deep breaths. Simply keep your breathing as natural as possible and try to stay relaxed throughout.

RHYTHMIC BREATHING

Rhythmic breathing, a meditation drawn from Yoga, helps you integrate the rhythms of your body: your pulse and your breathing. Feel your heart rate by placing your fingers on your wrist to take your pulse. Count six beats, one to six, then repeat until the rhythm becomes fixed in your mind. Next, turn your attention to your breathing. Sit in a comfortable posture, with your back straight, shoulders open, hands resting gently on your lap. This exercise is most successfully performed when your rib cage and chest are not drawn in but are kept relaxed and flexible.

Gently inhale a complete breath (from the previous exercise), counting six beats paced to your pulse. Hold your breath for three counts, then exhale slowly through your nose, counting six pulse beats. Repeat, breathing gently in this way.

SENSORY AWARENESS

The mind-body link is a primary bond. You can turn your attention to your body experience directly. Throughout this book we use body meditations to help with many areas of self-improvement.

You can perform this meditation lying down, sitting up, or standing. Each gives you a different experience. Practice all three so that you can apply any one to later meditations.

Begin by lying flat on your back on a wooden floor, mat, rug, or the grass outdoors. Rest your hands by your side on the floor, palms up. Close your eyes. Scan through your body with your attention. What this means is notice sensations, starting with your feet and moving up through all parts of your body. Notice how long your legs are, how far it is between your shoulder blades. Do you notice any tightness in your muscles? How does your body meet the floor? Feel the temperature of your skin. Keep your attention focused on your body. Let go of any other thoughts. Continually bring your mind back to your body. When you are ready, open your eyes and stretch.

FREE FLOW OF THE UNCONSCIOUS MIND

You have now experimented with focusing your mind on various things: a color, music, a memory, your breathing, and your body sensations. Another method of meditation reaches into the recesses of the unconscious by allowing the free flow of experience, without focusing the mind at all. By not focusing on anything in particular, you develop an inner sensitivity as you become aware of subtle cues from the back of your mind. For example, you have had times when you were deeply involved in a conversation on the telephone. After you hung up, you noticed many drawings ("doodles") created unconsciously while you were talking. This free flowing of hand movement occurred out of awareness, spontaneously, without any censorship or limitations from the conscious mind. In a similar way, the following exercises help develop this natural capacity through meditation.

FREE FLOW OF ATTENTION EXERCISE

Sit in a comfortable chair and lean back, relaxed. Close your eyes and allow your body to relax. Let your thoughts drift. Do not think about anything in particular. Relax your breathing, but do not direct your breaths in any particular way. You do not need to think of anything or do anything in particular. Simply wait, open-minded, wondering what your unconscious mind would like to present. Sometimes people feel as if they are floating, sometimes sinking. You might experience warmth or coolness, or perhaps an image will come to mind. Do not *try* to have any particular experience, simply allow what is. When you are finished, open your eyes and stretch.

The skills that are developed in this type of meditation are often so subtle that people do not notice them at first. The experience may be very slight, but by keeping an open and encouraging attitude, along with practice and training, you will eventually be pleasantly surprised. In the next exercise you can apply these skills more specifically.

ATTENTION TO YOUR HANDS

Sit in a chair, with both your feet flat on the floor. Let your hands rest on your legs, palms down. Close your eyes. Direct your attention to your hands. Applying the same open-ended approach as in the previous exercise, and wonder what you might experience in your hands. Will they feel light or heavy? Warm or cool? Perhaps you might notice a tingling in your fingertips. Ask yourself whether one hand feels lighter or heavier, warmer or cooler, or more tingly than the other. Allow any differences to occur, and observe carefully. Enjoy the experience. When you are ready, return to scanning outwardly. Open your eyes and stretch.

YIN-YANG: THE POINT BETWEEN

There is a point that is yin and yang and not yin and not yang, neither something nor nothing, a balance point between, where we find Oneness. Here with mind, body, and spirit in harmony, all flows naturally: the middle way. The Zen artist finds these moments when engaged in a Zen art. We experience such moments when we are in synchrony; then thought and action are one.

Each person can discover his or her unique balance of comfortable everyday functioning. For one person it may be when very active and busy, for another when calm and slow. This balance point may change at different periods of life and even with the seasons. Wherever your balance point may be, you find yourself living well, relaxed and at ease with yourself. The meditations that follow in Part Three help you function better in many areas of life and thereby discover and live with Oneness.

PART THREE
Applications

Life's challenges await us
Though we cannot control our fate
We can meet contingency hopefully
As we step through Destiny's gate.
— C. Alexander Simpkins

The meditation traditions of Eastern philosophy encourage us to recognize the potential within ourselves. Zen maintains that we are all Buddha. We can expand our potential and find the peace of enlightenment within by our own efforts. Solutions to life's challenges are waiting for your discovery. Meditation can light the way on the path.

By meditating as often as is required, you will begin to feel a transformation: new options unfold. You gain more flexibility and energy, calm, and an ever-developing harmony and trust of your inner self.

8

HABIT CHANGE: CREATING AND UNCREATING

"Habit a second nature! Habit is ten times nature," the Duke of Wellington is said to have explained, and the degree to which this is true no one probably can appreciate as well as one who is a veteran soldier himself. The daily drill and the years of discipline end by fashioning a man completely over again, as to most of the possibilities of his conduct.

—William James

H abits can work for you or against you. Most people have some habits they wish they could change and others they want to maintain. Habits involve many different behaviors, such as using bad language, watching too much television, being messy, driving too fast, nail-biting, smoking, overeating, and so forth. Habits can be positive as well, like exercise, good nutrition, healthy sleep patterns, organization, cleanliness, and so on. Meditation can help you disentangle yourself from negative habits and form new ones that are positive.

WHAT IS A HABIT?

Habits are actions that you do with regularity and relative consistency. It is difficult to imagine a habit that does not involve action. Another component of habits is that they are performed without awareness, automatically.

Sometimes habits derive from what is innate, being part of your nature or inherited from your ancestors. Habits may also be learned, evolving out of experiences you have had. Both types can be changed.

Action is a response to a perceived situation. Your interpretation of what you experience is primary. The meaning of your life situation is not thrust upon you, forced by circumstances. You create a personal meaning of events (what they mean to you) by your interpretation of what they are, however compelling the circumstances may be. Freud believed that the reality principle supersedes the pleasure principle in the mature, sane individual. We must seek to be open-minded in our interpretations.

Meditation practice helps show that reality is not easily confined to only one limited interpretation. Meditation gives you awareness of your habitual actions; and with this new awareness, you can gain control. This may help you free yourself for new possibilities. As you advance in your meditation, you learn how to approach what you want to change with an open, clear mind, without preconceived ideas or solutions.

CHANGING A TROUBLESOME HABIT

Meditation on the details of your life through careful focus of attention can bring about intense awareness and, consequently, more efficient performance of tasks. Meditative practice involves concentrating on actions and sensory details throughout the day, from the time when you get up in the morning to the time when you go to sleep at night, paying attention and thinking of an objective description of what you are doing as you do it.

EXERCISE IN MEDITATIVE AWARENESS

As you sit at the breakfast table, pay attention and think, Now I am sitting, now I am breathing, and so on. Stay with the continuum of awareness and strive to describe what you are doing, just as it is, without evaluation, except for your personal feelings (such as I am tasting it; it tastes bitter, sweet, etc.; I am enjoying the taste; I dislike it; and so on). As you are eating, think, Now, I am eating, I am biting, I am chewing, I am aware of noticing chewing, I am drinking my coffee (or my orange juice), and so on. Substitute the appropriate nouns and verbs for whatever habit you are noticing with awareness so that you are in touch with what you are doing as you do it, at the actual moment of doing it. This focus of attention is important. Do not seek to add to what you perceive in your experience, but if you discover that you unintentionally do so, then describe this action as well. The point is to stay with what is and to let go of each moment before.

The beginning of controlling any habit is to make it conscious, starting with paying close attention to the action. The habit must be described carefully and observed, with all its attendant antecedents and consequences. If you want to stop overeating, nail-biting, watching too much television, and such you should carefully describe and observe what it is and how you do it. Perhaps take notes in a journal each day. Another possible method is to describe what you do into a tape recorder as you do it. Engage in the activity normally. You will find yourself very conscious of the habit. Try not to be self-conscious, just aware. The following exercise shows you how to apply the previous meditative exercise to a habit you wish to change.

HABIT MINDFULNESS EXERCISE

Perform the habitual action as usual, with no change but with complete mental focus. Start by noticing how it feels to engage in your habit. How do you do it? When do you do it? What are the circumstances? Focus your attention on the action, just as it is; be as fully aware of the experience as you can be at the moment. Use the same skills you developed in meditating on the present moment, being fully aware of the habitual action. Do not attempt at first to change anything. Just observe, follow your actions, and experience what you are doing each moment, as if that moment were the first moment, every time. This begins the undoing of doing.

WORKING WITH RESISTANCE

Did you have difficulty staying with your moment-to-moment experience? If so, try the following exercises.

DISTRACTIONS EXERCISE

What prevents you from being aware, moment to moment? What distracts or attracts your attention? How do you get sidetracked? Do you find yourself watching something else, losing interest, thinking a series of thoughts? Try following that thought awhile before returning to your task.

FREE OF THOUGHT MEDITATION

Picture yourself meditating free of any distraction, focused and calm, with your mind still. What do you look like? How do you feel? What is the room like when you are free of thought? Do you find the center point of consciousness, neither here nor there, being at ease with not thinking conceptually, but not trying not to think, either?

TO DO OR NOT TO DO: THAT IS THE QUESTION

In deep meditation, there is no automatic habit of doing or not doing. Instead, you have a choice. This mental attitude removes obstacles because the habit is no longer automatic, and thus, out of your control.

We learn and we unlearn. There is, naturally, both yin and yang. What we do when we use conscious awareness, we can *not* do; what we make, we can *not* make. This general frame of mind is part of the background for an open attitude. The "not doing" approach frees you for an alternative choice.

EXERCISE IN NOT DOING I

Take the time to breathe carefully and with awareness as you smoke. Meditate on each breath as you sit or lie down, calmly. In and out, visualize yourself calm and relaxed without a cigarette. Try a "pause breath" between inhaling and exhaling. Lengthen the pause at times. Put the cigarette down and leave it, unfinished sometimes.

For dieters, pause between bites. Visualize yourself calm and relaxed without food. Leave some food on your plate at

Exercise in Not Doing I, continued

the end of the meal. You can follow the same logic with any habit. Experiment with not doing at intervals. Because of the unity between yin and yang, the more you repeat a response (such as "not doing") the more you build up inhibition until it disintegrates as a habit and is unlearned.

An artisan was trying to alter her habit of finishing a project poorly. She sanded incompletely and ignored the details, telling herself that it was fine without checking carefully. Often she tried to change this habit by finishing well but found that she inevitably slipped back into the negative habit. She used meditation to correct it. First, she thought about all the ways that she maintained this habit, such as hurrying and sanding in a curve that crossed the grain. Next, rather than trying to finish the project well, she simply tried not doing the negative things. She found that the whole action improved: the box was finished nicely, not by trying to do so but by not doing it badly.

EXERCISE IN NOT DOING II

What are all (or most of) the things you do that maintain a particular habit? Think about them carefully. List them if you need to. Once you have them clearly in mind, do not do these things. Keep your attention on the things you are *not* doing, to change the habit indirectly.

It is paradoxical that simply not performing an action you wish to stop, with attention and awareness, tends to make it less likely that it will recur as a habit. The intention to be aware gives you a choice.

MEANING

The concepts that you use to describe a habit can enhance or limit your ability to control your behavior. Smoking can be a habit that comes to mean many things to the smoker. For many people, smoking symbolizes relaxation, a moment away from work. Similarly, eating has many meanings to the overeater. Overeating can be a way to reduce tension. Each habit has certain meanings to the individual.

Buddhism teaches us to recognize that the meaning is not the thing itself. It is a construction of the mind and, therefore, unreal. The concept should not be mistaken for the habit itself. When you can recognize the meaning that you give to your habit and can separate the habit from its meaning, the compulsion to engage in the habit diminishes.

EXERCISE IN MEANING

Think about your habit. What does it do for you? What do you get out of it? What does it mean to you? If your answer is that it relaxes you, can you be relaxed without it? Think of relaxing. Can you recognize that the habit is not intrinsically relaxing, but that you have created this meaning for yourself? Can you imagine another way to relax (for instance, using the methods described earlier)? Whatever your habit, whatever the meaning for you, try by thought to separate the two.

HABITS AND THE ONENESS

Habit is a function of your system of actions related to your whole being; yet, at the same time, you can change an individual habit. How you interpret your situation affects what you do about it. Strengthen your awareness of your place in the Oneness, and you will find that you can make changes in your relationship with it.

MEDITATION ON ONENESS

This exercise is best done out in nature: a park, beach, woods, or garden. Sit down directly on the ground, with your legs crossed. Close your eyes. Place your hands flat on the ground. Feel the solidity, the mass. Notice how your weight is supported by the ground. Pay attention to how you meet the ground. Do you pull away or relax into it? After a while, bring your hands up into your lap and sit up straight. Feel the air around you, the sun on your skin. Smell the fragrance of the air. Notice how your breaths, in and out, are an interaction with your surroundings. Finally, clear your mind and be fully there.

You and the world are one. Therefore, seek appropriate circumstances to encourage the new habit you want to acquire or to discourage the old habit that you wish to break. If you have a problem with overeating, for example, do not fill the refrigerator with foods that you love to eat to excess. Do not linger at the supermarket with money in your pocket, or in the area of the store that sells all your favorite foods. Do not cook in massive proportions or have them cooked for you. Do not tempt yourself with stimuli, such as advertisements for your favorite food and so forth, that may weaken your resolve and help make it less likely that you will indulge in the habit you wish to break.

THE MIDDLE WAY

Yin and yang are at war within you when you wish to change something. Do not allow the one to dominate the other. Thus, true to Taoism, do not tip the balance from one to the other. Do not refuse to eat in order to master the impulse to overeat. Find the balance point, find the middle way; then you can change. Do not give in to your previous habit or, if you do, return as quickly as you can to the new one you wish to cultivate. Strengthen and increase the new whenever possible.

Sometimes unhealthy habits arise from efforts to do something positive. For example, smokers often use cigarettes to relax. Relaxation is healthy, even though smoking is not. You should look for positive, healthy actions to practice regularly. Make a consistent routine. Meditation can be primary, but you may want to take up a new activity for enjoyment and relaxation. The following guidelines can help you in the process. Think about these possibilities.

EXERCISE IN VISUALIZING CHANGE

What is a hobby or fun thing that you like and can imagine doing that would satisfy, in a more beneficial way, the same needs as your habit does? Think of a potentially positive activity that is doable, that you could imagine being enjoyable and meaningful. It is usually best to take on one that does not take too long. Is it taking a break at the office? Perhaps you could take up reading a short story instead of smoking. Or maybe you have a creative side that is aching to find expression. Is it cooking a new dish, building something out of wood or metal, or perhaps drawing a picture? You might like fixing something that matters to you or to someone else. For some people, eating may actually express a wish to share time doing something together with friends or family. Imagine the activity and visualize doing it regularly. But do not do it yet. Visualize in vivid detail, engaging as many of your senses as you can. See yourself there. Pay attention to what you feel, hear the sounds, notice whatever is associated with this activity. Repeat this exercise several times, until you feel ready to move forward. Then go on to the next exercise.

EXERCISE IN CHANGING A HABIT

Try to begin now, to take up a new positive habitual action, one that does not demand a lot but benefits you or others that matter to you. What is your resistance to doing it? Do you feel tired? Do you make up excuses? Do you forget? Does something else demand your attention? Do you suddenly find that you have to arrange your socks? Each time that you feel like doing the old habit, substitute the new one.

HABITS CAN BE GOOD FOR YOU!

Meditators cultivate good habits through routines, discipline, rituals, moral precepts, commitments. To be most effective, meditation should be practiced with consistency and regularity. Meditation and the meditative frame of mind become a habit. An attitude develops, a tendency to interpret events, behaviors, and circumstances in a way that is useful and positive.

> The great thing, then, in all education is to make our
> nervous system our ally instead of our enemy. . . . For
> this we must make automatic and habitual, as early as
> possible, as many useful actions as we can and guard
> against the growing into ways that are likely to be dis-
> advantageous to us, as we should guard against the
> plague. The more the details of our daily life we can
> hand over to the effortless custody of automatism, the
> more our higher powers of mind will be set free for their
> own proper work. (James 1918, 68)

Habitual actions are automatic, as stated earlier. We like to be able to turn over the control of our repeated actions to a kind of automatic pilot. Then we do not need to think about every action that we take, and we can be efficient. We merely think of the action that starts a particular sequence, and a whole chain of actions follows. Although the initial effort of altering a habit takes time, sitting regularly in meditation can become an automatic habit that requires little effort.

An experience that is regularly repeated tends to be learned, and what is noticed at the time tends to become a cue for what will be. This tendency may lead to learning, unintentionally, what should not be learned.

Habits can become bound to symbols, which are selected by attention. The symbol becomes a signal, a cue. We learn to meditate by practicing sitting. It should be an exacting way, fine-tuned to you individually—perhaps sitting on a cushion or on the floor, quietly, as our instructions in Part Two, "Meditation Basics," describe. After years and years of practice, just sitting cross-legged in position on a cushion on the ground tends to elicit a meditative mood. The position itself becomes a cue for the state of meditation.

THE VOW

In Buddhism, the vow, the commitment to the precepts, is always central. You can incorporate a level of commitment in bringing about a positive change. Always act decisively. Whenever you can, enact the new behavior, perform the action you want to do. If you want to diet, whenever you feel the urge, do it! If you have decided to be less messy, clean when you get the urge. Develop your energy and drive by just doing it, whenever you can.

9
INTELLIGENCE:
DEVELOPING THE TOOLS
TO USE IT

Returning to the root
We get the essence.

—Zen poem

DIFFERENT MENTAL TOOLS OF
EASTERN PHILOSOPHIES

M editation offers various approaches to developing your mind. The disciplines of Yoga, Buddhism, Zen, and Taoism all develop the mind in unique ways.

Some electroencephalograph (EEG) studies have shown that Yoga and Zen are not identical in how they alter brain functioning. Experienced Zen monks, Yogis, and students of these disciplines participated in a study of the neurophysiological and clinical aspects of mystical states of consciousness (Gelhorn and Kiely 1973, 484–90). The study found that with their eyes open, Zen monks and Yogi adepts produce rhythmic alpha waves in their brain during meditation. They could also produce rhythmic theta waves, usually a characteristic of deep sleep. These are very unusual brain waves for awake subjects.

The Yogis did not seem disturbed by stimuli at all, meditating deeply with no alteration of their brain's electrical activity during distraction from clicks and light. Through it all they continued to produce alpha waves, remaining undisturbed, calm, still meditating. The Yogis were actually unaware of the attempts to distract them. Yoga teaches how to withdraw from the outward direction of the senses, to focus inward toward higher consciousness.

Yoga can help you transcend the physical to experience other realms of consciousness. This has its specific uses as well. Swami Rama was able to demonstrate amazing control of his involuntary functions, such as heart rate, blood pressure, and so on, at the Menninger Clinic in Kansas. He dramatically showed it is possible to control functions that previously were considered involuntary, an ability available to all of us if we are willing to learn to develop it.

Zen monks were aware of, but did not habituate to (get accustomed to), the attempts to disturb the electrical activity of their brain by clicking noises from the experimenter. Their alpha rhythm remained undisturbed. Zen meditation quiets the cortex: there is less excitation, enabling the capacity to experience each stimulus for what it is. The habituation that would normally be expected did not occur.

Zen Buddhism is first and foremost an experience grounded in the here and now. Thought is secondary. The primary effort is to let go of abstract concepts and experience each moment anew. Zen bypasses the intellect in favor of direct experience. A change in perspective results in the mind's opening up to creative thought.

We cannot use Zen to develop the intellect. Zen is antitheoretical and derogates mere worldly unenlightened intellectual understanding. But we can clear away mistaken thought processes, improving how the intellect functions. Yoga encourages focusing attention through the mind, to withdraw from the world's limited reality as perceived through the senses. Awareness not engaged in the illusory world of the senses becomes available for a higher reality, the universal Oneness. Taoism, although not a part of these research studies, also offers its own mental skills, to become more aware of inner rhythms and at one with what is. Each philosophy has its own approach that you can learn to use in the exercises throughout this book.

ENHANCING INTELLECTUAL FUNCTIONING

Intelligence is often thought of as a fixed quantity, the IQ, a quality of mind that is a given, stable and unchanging. The classical, standard intelligence test developed by Wechsler, known as the WAIS (Wechsler Adult Intelligence Scale), has shown that measurements of intelligence remain relatively stable throughout a person's lifetime. The capacity to perform intellectual tasks such as repeating block-pattern designs, solving arithmetic problems, remembering items, and defining vocabulary terms increases up to somewhere from five years of age to the early twenties, then changes little until old age, when a gradual decline takes place.

In daily life, intelligence varies greatly based on how well people use the intelligence they have. The expression of intelligence, its functional use, can be addressed and improved, regardless of what the capacity of intelligence is. For our purposes, the aspect of intelligence that we can alter is its practical application. Like the Pragmatists, we can think of intelligence in terms of results rather than as a fixed datum. Intelligence researchers foresaw the potential of functional intelligence:

INTELLIGENCE: DEVELOPING THE TOOLS TO USE IT

> *Intelligence is an attribute of a person's performance,*
> *that is, an attribute of his past or current behavior, and*
> *it is not an unchanging or unchangeable attribute of the*
> *person. Changing conditions, personal or environmental*
> *. . . may increase or decrease the functional level of a*
> *person's relative level of demonstrable intellectual*
> *resources. (Matarazzo 1972, 21)*

Examples of how the expression of intelligence changes are all too apparent when we are having a bad day and nothing goes right. Another day comes and we are seemingly infallible, on track, at our best. We have moments of higher intelligence and, unfortunately, moments of lower intelligence as well.

Even at our best, we use about only 10 percent of our mental capacity; the rest is potential. How can we get access to this potential, to use more of this incredible capacity that we have? How can we get on track and stay there? What do we do to enhance our intelligence to its functional utmost?

One answer is clear: Meditation can help clear the mental decks of useless baggage and clutter, opening the way for efficient use of your intelligence. Like a computer, the mind can free its active RAM for processing information. With the tools of attention and concentration, your mind becomes focused and directed to the task at hand so that you can make the best use of your faculties. Meditation, like no other discipline, teaches us how to use these qualities of mind. It takes consistent effort, but the rewards are worthwhile and will ripple throughout the sea of your consciousness.

If you want to develop intellectual skills with meditation, start small, then expand from this base. Each success builds to another success, and soon your intellect is growing and your abilities are evolving—gradually at first, almost imperceptibly, but the small changes tend to snowball into larger ones in a chain reaction. This kind of application of meditation must be individualized, but these are some general guidelines to follow. Begin now to be what you want to be. Only now exists. Each event is reflected in another, and thus the seeds of the future are reflected in the present.

THE TOOL OF ATTENTION

To enhance our mental functioning, we can use our attention capacities. Attention can be conscious or unconscious. You can deliberately and consciously attend to an experience, as in some of these exercises. Sometimes you do not notice things consciously, yet you may still be attending to them unconsciously, receiving impressions for perception. Like conscious attention, unconscious attention is also a natural ability of all living organisms. Attention that is unconscious and "free-floating" can be useful in applying your meditation to developing your mind.

LEARNING TO FOCUS ATTENTION
CONSCIOUSLY

Attention is needed for anything to be consciously noticed. As a variation on the old philosophical conundrum, if a tree falls in a forest and no one pays attention, does anyone hear it? Conscious attention helps us notice and respond appropriately to circumstances.

A meditator can use many kinds of inner imagery as a focal point for concentration. It is easy to pay attention to what interests us, but this is not always possible, since we are often called upon to attend to things that are not especially interesting. Sketching an image, a symbol, helps. The wiring is there, but people do not realize this, and then do not use it.

CONSCIOUS ATTENTION EXERCISE

Find something that interests you naturally. If you like art, think about a favorite painting or sculpture. If sports interest you, recall an exciting game. Now link it to something else that you can also use with conscious control. For the art lover, think about a theory of art. With sports, consider the strategy used in that game. Then gradually you will begin to find your way into contemplation, with the potential of getting lost in the experience. Subjects you can easily contemplate will lead you to attend successfully to more complex, less interesting subjects.

LEARNING TO FOCUS ATTENTION UNCONSCIOUSLY

Human beings are not merely another form of biological machine, an organism that responds to a stimulus with a mechanical learned response. We are quickly bored when a situation requires us to be machinelike. We crave stimulation. We reach out for excitement and actively seek challenge, novelty, and problems to solve. Human nature is contrary and irascible. Something more is there, hidden in the wings, awaiting the call for its time to appear onstage. This is when the unconscious begins its positive work, resulting in a new synthesis emerging, one that is not limited to conscious boundaries.

Even daydreaming is not a waste of time. The daydream can be a doorway to deeper regions of your mind. You enter and find your way, through symbolism, to experiences that are important to you. Visual symbols give you an opportunity to react.

UNCONSCIOUS ATTENTION EXERCISE

Have you ever gotten lost in a moment of daydreaming or reverie? This is a doorway into unconscious attention. Have you ever spent a timeless moment deeply concentrating on something of inner significance, then suddenly snapped out of it, realizing you had not thought of where you were or what you were doing? This is a meditative trance, spontaneously begun. Seek a symbol that has personal significance and the potential to fascinate you. A mandala, an Escher picture, or any visual aid that is meaningful to you will do. Do not focus on it directly. Instead, let your thoughts drift freely as you look at it, allowing whatever comes to mind as you contemplate and focus deeply, so that your own thoughts and feelings can be stimulated.

It is positive and beneficial to be flexible and focused, with the capacity to pay full attention. Attention is also affected by different types of visual organization: diagrams, maps, and graphs can be objects for concentration, evoking your personal interest. Experiment.

DEVELOPING THINKING ABILITY

Zen Buddhism seeks to guide the meditator toward no-thought, empty mind. Most commonly if we try not to think, we find that we cannot. Thought follows thought in an endless sequence, a flowing river of ideas. The use of the mind seems automatic, with no escape.

The Rasa-Mandala (from the Bhagavata Purana).
Central India, Malwa.
Opaque watercolor on paper, c. 1690.
Edwin Binney III Collection. San Diego Museum of Art.

When you try not to think, you inevitably focus your attention on thinking; and whether you intend to or not, you often begin an inner battle, a battle for control of processes that you cannot control. This is akin to the law of reversed effort in hypnosis: the harder you try not to think about something, paradoxically, the more you think about it. The thinking process itself is the inroad into the empty mind. The first step is to turn your attention to thinking itself.

ATTENDING TO THINKING

Let us explore what we are doing at a particular moment when we think. Are we really thinking for a purpose, deeply contemplating? Or are we merely spinning our mental wheels? What are we doing? Focus your attention now on your own mind for a few moments. Consider whether you can instead embrace thinking itself, taking it seriously, permitting yourself to think. Meditate on thinking so that you are not really distracted by it.

FOLLOWING A THOUGHT TO ITS ROOTS EXERCISE

Observe each thought as it emerges, following it to its source, its logical assumptions, its roots. Try this with one idea or concept that matters to you. What is the origin of this thought? How do you know it is significant, of concern? Is there really a rational basis for this concern? Or is there instead no basis? What is the basis for it? What keeps it central to you? This is the general outline of the method of analysis of thinking that helps to dissolve it as a process. You may follow this through for a detailed, specific, individual concept, or you may go into the more general. Both methods have their use and application about a concept. Your thinking processes may change once freed from faulty bases.

FOLLOWING THOUGHT MEDITATION

Follow each thought, notice each thought as it arises, and then notice the next one. Try to maintain the vantage point as observer at the riverbank, watching. Do not lose yourself in any particular thought, but pay close attention to the process of your thinking.

When you think deeply, clearly, and carefully, the thought ceases to be a distracting problem. Superficial thought leads to problems. This is an ageless insight of Zen: that thinking will eventually slow down of its own, by reaching deeper thought. Sometimes we believe that we cannot think deeply at all, but it is really a matter of finding the natural wiring that we already have within ourselves. Buddhism calls this our Buddha mind. Thoughts are not to be feared. They are our inroad to our true nature.

RESISTANCE

Thinking also tends to draw your attention to things that pester you with conflict, to emotional issues, and to relationships with unsolved problems. Sometimes these thoughts are mere inklings, subtle and not clear in meaning. Try to follow such thoughts, without judgment, as far as you can. These thoughts can be inner signals, important keys to your deeper self. If you find that you cannot get anywhere with these meditations on thinking and that you continue to be bothered by thoughts, talking to a professional psychologist or counselor, especially one sympathetic to meditation, may be helpful.

10
LEARNING AND MEMORY: USING WISDOM TO GAIN KNOWLEDGE

To common sense nothing is more obvious than the fact that learning requires concentration, effort, sustained attention, or absorbing interest. If these conditions are present in sufficient degree we can learn almost anything.

—Gordon Allport

LEARNING

Your ability to learn can be enhanced by meditation. Whether you are a student in a structured program or a "student of life," you can learn how to learn, so that the material becomes easier to master. Meditation helps attune your mental tools to the task at hand for greater success.

LISTENING IN CLASS

Time spent studying at home can be streamlined. Learning comes more readily when the student fully absorbs material that is presented in the classroom. Taking notes and listening carefully are the customary tools and are good skills to develop. But sometimes you might become so intent on their mechanics that you miss the essence of the lecture. The following exercise, drawn from Taoism, helps you make the most of classroom learning.

MEDITATIVE LISTENING

Before you enter the classroom, relax your body and mind with a brief meditation. Open your senses to the moment and notice your skin, the sounds around you, your breathing. When you get to class, sit up straight but as comfortably as possible. Breathe gently. Pay attention to the sound of the professor's voice. Notice when he or she seems to give special emphasis and write this down in your notes. Do not concentrate on each detail as an isolated unit but listen more deeply to the organization and sense of what is being communicated. Allow yourself to receive the material for what it is, not for what it can do for you.

READING COMPREHENSION

Reading comprehension, one of the functional applications of intelligence, can be improved by searching for and perceiving the significant relationships among ideas and concepts. Many tutoring and learning programs are founded on this belief. The interrelationship of all things is a fundamental enlightened construct of Yoga, Zen, Buddhism, and Taoism: the Oneness. Mindfulness of this interrelationship stimulates associations of ideas, leading to concepts in one frame of reference, to theory in another. There are partial unities, subcategories that have their place in the universal Oneness. Unity is within an interrelationship, not outside it.

If reading comprehension depends on grasping the interrelationships of concepts as well as understanding the intended meanings, then tools that apply your mind to noticing these relationships will help you develop the ability to read well. In one study, vocabulary scores were found to improve when children drew simple diagrams of new words' definitions. Another study used familiar stories as a representational context for generating links with new information. This approach is also the basis of mnemonic memory systems.

INTERRELATIONSHIP EXERCISE I

This meditation is best done sitting comfortably, with your eyes closed or slightly open (whichever way allows you to delve into your mind). Take a few moments to become attuned to your body and mind as you sit. Feel your presence within. Then notice your skin and how you meet the floor or chair. Now expand your awareness to include the space around you. Notice the details, and experience yourself within it, as part of it. Consider how the air you breathe has been a part of this space and how it now enters your lungs to be cycled through your body. Expand your awareness outward to include the building, the other people in it, then the entire area, the city and all its inhabitants, the country, the planet, and out to the farthest reaches of your imagination of our universe.

INTERRELATIONSHIP EXERCISE II

Now that you have meditated on your interrelationship with the greater whole, apply this meditation to the subject you are trying to comprehend. For example, if you are studying chemistry, begin with the subatomic units and expand outward to contemplate the chemical structure of the universe and how intricately objects are interrelated. If you are studying a literary work, contemplate the plot, style, etc., of the particular work. Meditate on the period in which it was written; then generalize to writings of this type, perhaps even to the meaning of literature in general. In all these applications, take the time to search for many subtle interrelationships.

CREATIVE LEARNING

The key quality of creativity is the ability to detach your mind from habitual, established patterns of thought and to apply new variations. Through meditation we learn to let go of set constructs, to recognize that things are not what they seem. Transformation into other forms is basic to creative thinking.

Use your meditative skills to transform something into another form. A Zen story illustrates the point. To a new student of Zen, mountains are mountains and rivers are rivers. In the midst of Zen study, mountains are no longer mountains and rivers are no longer rivers. After enlightenment, mountains are once again mountains and rivers are once again rivers. The ability to take the situation apart analytically and put it back together again brings about a greater depth of understanding.

Train your mind by deconstructing an object into its different parts and then reproducing the pattern as a whole.

MEDITATION IN DIFFERENTIATION AND REUNIFICATION

Find a simple household object, such as a table, a potted plant, a fan. Look at it closely, noticing all the parts and how it is put together. Close your eyes. Picture the object. Then experiment with taking it apart mentally. When you have it in several pieces, try to put the pieces back together again in a new way. Some people may want to draw it on paper. Others may prefer to do the entire meditation in their head. Finally, reassemble it as it was originally. Open your eyes and look at the real object. Do you see it differently now?

VARIATION

Using additional senses can be helpful. Touch the object. Notice the textures, the temperature of the object. Look at its colors. Does it have a perfume or scent? The added dimension of other senses gives you more detail for your imagery.

CREATIVE THINKING EXERCISE

This exercise helps you discover a new alternative. Write the problem down. Translate it into simple language. Restate it, either mathematically or graphically with a picture. Classify it. Then turn it upside down. When an idea comes to you, write it down. Look for a seemingly irrelevant factor in the problem situation or perhaps a seemingly unrelated pattern in your own mind.

EXERCISING FREEDOM FROM
REDUNDANT PATTERNS

Clearing the mind corrects mental blocks to problem-solving and stimulates the use of analogy in creating a new solution. Your mind can be cleared both by emptying and by filling it when you scan relevant information to the point of redundancy. Then, suddenly, insightful discoveries may come.

Clearing the mind helps free you from excessive analysis of useless data and from narrow classifications that limit understanding; then spontaneous discovery occurs. Spontaneity is a key element to intelligent use of memory. The best memory recall is natural and spontaneous, effortless. If you are seeking insight to help you solve a creative problem and you are stuck, try this method, drawn from meditation.

DISCOVERY MEDITATION

Begin by clearing your mind in preparation. Use the clearing the mind exercises in Part Two, "Meditation Basics." Sit for at least five minutes to set the stage. Then immerse yourself fully in the data. Concentrate on it: read, think, surround yourself with it imaginatively, including visual and auditory sources if possible, even books and articles, night and day, until you are at one with it. Then step back from the selective process of attention, of fixing your concentration on the information, and let your attention wander. Observe your reactions and insights. Tell your ideas to someone who is willing to listen. Say them into a tape recorder, key them into a computer or typewriter, or draw them. Find a way to record them until you run out of ideas and insights. Now clear your mind again and

> **Discovery Meditation, continued**
> contemplate the nothingness. This will be easier after running
> out of ideas. Wait. A spontaneous image or symbol may
> occur to you. Note it somehow. It may be a useful insight, re-
> leased by your unconscious. It is not infallible, but often you
> discover something new. The important thing is the medita-
> tive mode. Do not reason with the image or analyze it at first.
> Let it be. Concentrate and, staying in the center, allow your
> creative discoveries to evolve.

MEMORY

The activity of the great way is vast;
It is neither easy nor difficult.

—Zen poem

Memory is also a primary factor in learning. Students are constantly
stretching the limits of memory. The three Rs of remembering are
recording, retaining, and retrieving. First, we acquire the material,
then we place it in mental storage. From there, it is available to be retrieved for use. If the material is needed much later, it goes into long-
term memory. An example of a long-term memory is remembering
the teacher you had for math class or perhaps English when you were
a freshman in high school. Short-term memory is for those things that
are most recent, such as what you ate for breakfast today. Improving
any aspect of the three Rs improves memory.

Part of learning involves memorization of data. It is always easier
to remember one or two things. When you begin to have a large number of items to recall, memory falls off. The journey of a thousand
miles begins with one step. Zen shows us how the world we experience is created by our mind. You can make and unmake an object in

ways that make it easier to remember. The following exercise helps you apply this technique to learning.

EXERCISE IN MAKING AN OBJECT

Break down into little bits the material you are trying to master. Reorganize it again into smaller bits of information; then master each one, linking them in a chain. To memorize something, unmake the subject of study and let a new unity create itself. Apply this process to anything you want to memorize. A series that is related to you personally is easier to recall. You can create your own relationship through similarities, first letter, opposites—anything that you find meaningful or even humorous.

EXERCISE IN UNMAKING AN OBJECT

Zen points out that objects are constructions of the mind: they neither are nor are not. You do not have to "make" anything. Then there is no problem; you simply "do it." You do your work or your study without thinking of an object or purpose or goal, but with mindfulness. Held exactly in the moment of doing it, you are lost in the action, the doing.

Approach your study session with this orientation—for example, without thinking of the threat of a test or of not understanding the material. Do not make anything of it; just study. Nothing else need exist. Problems vanish. Blocks to studying can vanish. And before you realize it, you have learned the material.

MAKE A SYMBOL

When you use a symbol, you can memorize material and then set it aside to recall later. This symbol becomes a mental cue, like a computer icon, to recall the information when you need it.

MENTAL CUE EXERCISE

Imagine a circle. Put the information that you want to remember inside it. Clear your mind and visualize the circle with the information inside it. You can use this device to remember something, by setting a cue.

INTERFERENCE WITH MEMORY

Memory can be interfered with, and this interference causes forgetting. A common example is someone's interrupting you when you are about to say something, which causes you to forget what you were going to say. Material from classes may be forgotten when students have to rush from one lecture to the next. Meditation teaches us to pause and take a moment between experiences.

MEDITATIVE REVIEW

After a study session or a class, sit quietly in meditation. Allow yourself to imaginatively revisit the lesson. If it was a lecture, rehear the professor speak. After a classroom discussion, recall what was said. After studying, go over the material, perhaps picturing it, maybe recalling the data or reviewing the ideas. This meditative review can be done in just a few minutes. The time spent helps you make the learning a part of you.

An item that is similar to another that you want to memorize can also interfere with its recall. When studying complex material, labels can be confusingly alike. Meditation helps you reach beyond the label, to the information itself.

OVERCOMING FORGETFULNESS

Many people are plagued with forgetfulness. They find themselves forgetting where they placed their keys or their glasses or the name of someone they just recently met. There are ways to work with your mind, using your meditative skills, to change this forgetful tendency.

You can work with your memory by utilizing focused attention and concentration in meditation. Taoism's attitude of allowing, permitting, and staying evenly poised in the center becomes useful. When you wait, patiently and expectantly, the stage is set for memory to do its work in recalling.

REMEMBERING A NAME OR AN ITEM FROM THE INNER MIND

Concentrate on your feeling about the name or the item that you cannot recall. You may have a sense of it being on the tip of your tongue or just outside the reach of your consciousness. Accept this, with faith that the knowledge or the memory exists because you knew it at one time. Wait patiently with your mind clear. With confidence that it will come into your mind later, go on to something else. You have set your inner mind to work on remembering. When you least expect it, the memory will occur to you.

The next exercise uses the capacity of the mind to reexperience or recall things through their unity or Oneness. Within each experience, any part implies the whole, and the whole implies its parts. The context, the time, the situation at any given moment, are part of a larger unity. Data can be retrieved when viewed in its larger context: as details that are an indivisible part of the whole.

RECALL USING MENTAL CUES

First, take some time to clear your mind, and then search for the point where you feel the data is just not quite being recalled by you, barely outside the range of your consciousness. Search now for a symbol, a letter of the name, the size of the object, the approximate shape, or the color. Now wait, allowing your pointed concentration to waver so that your attention drifts and shifts a bit. The whole may be drawn into view, with the individual parts: they are linked as one. A remembered context helps—for example, a facial detail of a person whose name you are trying to recall. The image of the face, the sound of the voice—anything can help you remember the experience. Sometimes an associated or similar memory comes first.

If you are seeking to remember directions to a house, start with the vague feeling. What do you recall? Then free-associate, to see if names of streets pop into your mind. Finally, clear your mind of concepts, to await its filling with the recollection.

When you do recall what you are searching for, pause. Concentrate on it and appreciate it. Be grateful to your inner mind for releasing it to you. Each time you do this, success builds on success, and you will find it easier to recall the next time. When you are reaching beyond your usual range, permit the vague, general impression or feeling to come. Accept it, knowing that it may mature into the complete recalled memory.

REMEMBERING NAMES

Has this ever happened to you? You are at a party and are introduced to someone new. You move on to talk to others, giving the meeting little thought. Later on in the evening, your new acquaintance speaks to you. Much to your embarrassment, you have forgotten his or her name.

Memory is influenced by emotional factors. If you like or dislike something you are trying to remember, that feeling influences how easily you can recall it. The face and name of your best friend or worst enemy is a lot easier to recall than that of someone you hardly know or care about, even though you might have seen that person regularly in going about your daily life and heard his or her name as well.

The disciplined focus of mind that meditation brings can help prevent this kind of situation.

EXERCISE IN NAME RECALL

At the time of introduction, listen to the name, ask the person to repeat it, restate the name, and then use it once or twice. Think of the face and the name, or a quality of the person, and associate them together mindfully. The Oneness of person and world is a reality. Later, when you are trying to recall the name, remember where you were when you met, the circumstances, the time. Picture the scene vividly. Wait calmly for the name to pop into your mind.

Learning and memory are enhanced when you can approach life with greater awareness. By making meditation a part of everyday life, you will find yourself naturally remembering what you need to know.

11
EMOTIONS:
THE BALANCE POINT

Our Nature is the mind. And the mind is our nature.
—Bodhidharma

E motions and moods are part of everyone's life. We care about what we feel. Most events that occur during the course of the day involve some type of feeling tone. Even if these feelings come and go, the experience at the time may be very vivid. Being comfortable with your feelings and emotions not only helps you feel better but can actually improve many aspects of your life.

If you are disturbed by your moods and emotions, meditation can help you find your center. Eastern philosophy offers a unique perspective that can be incorporated through meditation. The exercises in this chapter present many different ways to apply meditation to your emotional life.

If you find that nothing you do seems to make a difference and that your feelings are interfering with your life, psychotherapy may be appropriate. Moods and strong recurring emotions can stem from deep-rooted problems for which psychotherapy may be appropriate, because of the personal nature of these feelings. Psychotherapy can be useful in such circumstances, particularly when there is a positive rapport between therapist and client. If this is the case, meditation can also be used as an adjunct to the psychotherapeutic process and may help your therapy progress in many ways. Alternatively, after therapy has helped resolve worldly conflicts, the path of meditation may be open to you. Others may find that meditation is sufficient in itself and resolves the specific through resolving the general. There are no standardized routes to follow to enlightenment.

ATTITUDES

Where do emotions come from? Attitudes are the primary source of many emotions. An attitude is "a relatively stable affective response to an object" (Insko 1967, 2). Attitudes lead to a readiness to respond to objects or symbols of objects in a certain way.

Attitudes often form early in childhood. We have many experiences that we interpret as meaning something to us personally, that influence how we feel. Some we remember and know consciously, but many go into the unconscious mind to affect our responses without our being in touch with the links. Whether conscious or unconscious, attitudes are a state of mind, often emotionally laden, that tend to remain stable.

Jerome D. Frank, M.D., a researcher at Johns Hopkins University Medical School, developed a conceptual framework that explains emotions based on the concept of attitudes. "All human behavior reflects the need to make sense of the world" (Frank and Frank 1991,

24). We create a meaningful environment through our experiences. Emotions as well as behaviors and thoughts are influenced by these attitudes.

Brain research confirms that our perceptions of the world are mediated by meaning and interpretation. Researcher Michael Gazzaniga points out that there is a part of the brain, the "interpreter," that constructs theories to explain why behavior occurs (Gazzaniga 1978). The theories and concepts we construct about our experiences influence how we feel and what has meaning to us. Zen discipline intends to stop any theorizing and interpreting that is external to living in meditation.

ENERGY

According to Pierre Janet, a famous nineteenth-century French psychologist who became a renowned authority on psychotherapy, energy and mind are the primary forces behind emotional difficulties. He believed that problems with feelings derive from an underlying disturbance in energy, leading to characteristic types of mental activity. Some people suffer from too little energy, resulting in problems like depression, apathy, and chronic fatigue. Others have too much energy, finding themselves burdened with fits of anger and sadness. Janet advocated treatment that brought about the opposite condition, through excitation or relaxation therapies.

> *Rightly or wrongly, I believe that both psychological science, and psychotherapy which has to make a practical application of psychology, can derive great benefit from the study of those characteristics of behavior which may*

be termed the grades of psychological energy and psy-chological tension, and also from the study of the various oscillations of mental activity. (Janet 1925, 1914)

Many problems are merely attempts by patients to reduce or increase their energy. The goal of treatment was to restore vital energy to its natural balance.

Chinese acupuncture is based on the application of yin-yang to chi. An emotional or physical problem is due to an excess, deficiency, or blockage of the flow of chi. Acupuncture helps restore the flow of chi by stimulating some points and removing blockages.

EXTREMES OF EMOTIONS

Researchers at Harvard Medical School have recently found a link between explosive anger and the risk of heart attacks. Sudden elevations in blood pressure add to the release of adrenaline and other hormones that raise the heart rate and blood pressure. These researchers recommended meditation as an effective way to lower the energy level that is aroused by intense anger (Williams 1994, 29).

At the other extreme, low energy can also present problems for daily life. Depression is one of the most common moods (affecting at least 10 percent of the population from time to time) behind many people's problems. The physical symptoms of depression are low energy, apathy, loss of appetite, or lack of interest in former pleasures. Doctors caution that when people are depressed, they are more susceptible to disease because of a lowered immune system response.

CALMING TO FIND A BETTER BALANCE

Practicing regular calming can be very helpful in combating extremes in energy and strong disturbing emotions. It is best to begin at a time when you do not feel the uncomfortable feeling, when you are feeling fairly level. Once you have developed and trained your skills in the habit of calmness, you can call on your ability to be calm in the midst of a strong emotion or just before it erupts, moderating the course of your usual reaction.

PROGRESSIVE BODY RELAXATION EXERCISE

You can identify when you are relaxed by contrast with when you are not. It is easier to notice differences. Contrasting the experience of loose muscles with that of tight muscles makes it easier to recognize when you are tense.

Lie down on your back on the floor, a firm bed, or couch. Let your whole body relax as deeply as you can. Then tighten your whole body, from head to foot. Hold this contraction for approximately thirty seconds. Then let go and relax all over. Notice the difference in your muscles from when they were tight. Repeat three times. With practice, you will gain greater control over your muscles, to be able to relax more deeply at will. Try to deepen your overall relaxation each time. You may rest awhile after producing this deep relaxation. Try to stay awake!

DIFFERENTIAL BODY RELAXATION EXERCISE

This exercise is more challenging. Practice helps you to relax one part of your body while holding another part tight. This is called differential relaxation and can be very useful at times when you need to exert some muscles but not others. Let all your muscles relax as much as possible. Now tighten your hands into fists. Allow your arms to be tight also, up to your shoulders. Keep the rest of your body as relaxed as possible. Hold this tightness for approximately thirty seconds. Notice how the contracted muscles of your arms and hands feel, and how they feel different from other, less tense, parts (such as your legs). Relax your arms and hands. Pay attention to how your arms and hands feel now that they are relaxed and compare this feeling in your mind with how they felt before. Repeat the tightening and relaxing of these specific areas. Next, tighten your neck, shoulders, and head. Grimace to tighten the muscles in your face and raise your shoulders, but keep your arms, back, chest, stomach, and legs relaxed. Hold for approximately thirty seconds. Release the tension and relax this area, making comparisons as before. Relax fully for about one minute, letting go of any tension you might notice. Repeat again, tighten and then relax. Follow the same procedure for your back and chest. Then do your lower area, down to your legs and feet. Try to keep all the surrounding muscles as relaxed as possible while tensing the targeted area. When you are finished with each separate section, tense your whole body: face, hands, arms, shoulders, midsection, lower body, legs, and feet. Hold for thirty seconds, then relax everywhere. Let go of all unnecessary tension. By repeating this exercise daily, after a while you will find that your control of muscle groups improves while the depth of your relaxation increases. This control helps you in life in many ways, as you get used to applying it.

RELAXATION AWARENESS EXERCISE

This exercise can be done at work or at home whenever you have an uninterrupted few minutes alone. Sit down—at your desk at work or on the floor if you have a private office or are at home. Close your eyes. Follow your breathing for a minute or so, letting yourself settle. Scan through your body with your inner attention and allow yourself to relax as much as possible. Notice whether you are holding tight the muscles of your face, neck, shoulders, or back. These are typical areas in which to hold tension. Can you release these areas? Don't think about anything in particular, except to be relaxed in the moment. After three to five minutes, open your eyes, stand up, and stretch if you can. Short breaks like this, taken here and there during your day, can help to make calmness a way of life.

Repeat these calming exercises frequently. You will find that calming meditations practiced here and there in your day will moderate excessive energy extremes so that you can moderate your moods and emotions more easily.

REDUCE RIGIDITY TO RELEASE ENERGY

People who are bothered by their emotions often feel stuck in rigid patterns. Rigidity can be linked to blocked chi, which brings about fatigue and lower energy. The Taoist sage knows how to bend like the willow, to be supple and flexible. The rigid oak must pit its strength against the stormy elements. It breaks if the conditions are too forceful, too extreme and intense. When people take an inflexible attitude toward difficulties, they do not cope as well as they could. Learn to bend like the willow, and you will bypass many difficulties and not let circumstances take you to the breaking point. When the difficulty passes, you can spring back again.

Meditative breathing helps you become more supple, less rigid. As Lao-tzu wrote in the *Tao te Ching*, "By concentrating your breath until you become soft, can you be like an infant?" (Duyvendak 1992, 36). Chuang-tzu spoke of breathing from your heels. This became a philosophical inspiration for tai chi. In the following exercise, the whole body moves as one, energy flows naturally, and vitality is raised.

WHOLE BODY BREATHING EXERCISE

Stand comfortably in your bare feet, socks, or slippers, with your feet approximately shoulder-width apart. Close your eyes and breathe comfortably. Follow the air as it goes in through your nose and down into your lungs. Imagine that with each breath in, the air penetrates through your entire body, softening and relaxing throughout. With each exhalation, tensions are released from head to toe.

Next, raise your hands lightly over your head while you breathe in, expanding your rib cage slightly as it fills with air. Let your arms drop back gently to your sides as you breathe out. Breaths and movements should be soft. Repeat several times.

LETTING GO OF
PROBLEMATIC CONSTRUCTS

Mental constructs are often the origin of many of our emotional reactions, as explained earlier. The enlightened mind need not rely on beliefs, opinions, and attitudes about situations to be oriented. This exercise helps you understand and then apply this principle.

"OPINIONS ARE EMPTY" EXERCISE

Consider an opinion, belief, or attitude you once held about someone or something in your life, but later changed. For example, perhaps you disliked someone but later, as you got to know this person better, found that you liked him or her. Or perhaps you followed one political party and then switched. Many people have experienced loving a particular food as a child (pizza, cotton candy, etc.) and found that later as an adult, such foods had lost their exciting appeal. Recall how certain you felt about your original opinion, how real it seemed to you at the time. Compare this with how you feel now, with your different opinion, taste, and so forth, concerning the same thing, yet just as certain, just as real.

If you set aside all the rationalizations for why you changed your mind, you might begin to realize that these opinions and tastes have no absolute reality of their own. And yet, based upon such opinions, certain emotions and reactions follow. All this seems very fixed at the time, but if you contemplate it from the neutral center point, you begin to recognize the transitory quality of such opinions, tastes, and beliefs.

CHANGE YOUR TEMPER

There was once a monk who came to Bankei, the famous seventeenth-century Japanese Zen master to help him tame his temper. He told Bankei, "I was born with a short temper, and there is nothing I can do about it. I'm hoping that your teachings will cure me."

Bankei answered, "Do you have your temper here now? Bring it out for me and I will cure it."

The monk answered, "I do not feel angry now. It just pops out when something provokes me."

Bankei answered, "You were not born angry. You create it yourself. You work yourself up. All of this is illusion. If you only could realize that you have a Buddha mind within, you will never lose your temper again."

Bankei believed that people create outbursts of temper when their senses are stimulated by something outside. These stimuli incite them to react against others or to assert their emotions. When people have no attachment to ego, they can be impartial. Then there is no anger. Bankei's solution was to live in what he called the "unborn Buddha mind." Then harmony and calm prevail (Waddell 1994, 61–62).

Having now contemplated beliefs and emotions, you can use your meditation to find a quiet center that is beyond judgment and beyond emotion, that balances yin and yang, within your own mind. For Zen and Taoism, the answer is to remain with your here-and-now awareness without conceptualization. Do not make yourself the center of the universe. Expand to include others. We do not need to take from others, to self-aggrandize. As Zen master Hui-neng taught, Nothing is missing. Rather, it is our additions, distractions, and conflicts of thought and emotion that hide this balance, misleading us into believing we are lacking a calm center. Meditation helps you reclaim your own natural resources.

EXERCISE IN THE UNBORN MIND

Take a walk. As you are walking, attend only to the experience. Notice your feet on the ground, the sights around you, the air on your face, the smells, the sounds. Do not think about or judge your walk in any way. Do not concern yourself with whether you think it is too noisy, too cold, too hot, too polluted. Simply walk and be involved with it. This is the unborn mind. If you can stay with it, in whatever you are doing, where is your anger?

EMBRACE YOUR MOOD

People often try to escape their moods, change them, or avoid them. Paradoxically, one of the most effective ways to be calmer and less volatile is to embrace your mood, your emotion, to feel it fully and become one with it. In this way, you come to know more about yourself. Then you have the opportunity to learn from what you feel. The following series of exercises draws on the skills you have already developed in meditative observation.

EXERCISE IN OBSERVATION OF EMOTIONS

In meditation you can watch your thoughts from the objective, unbiased vantage point of your inner mind. You can transfer this meditative ability of observation to your emotions. Perform this exercise at different times of the day, when you are feeling different emotions.

Sit comfortably. Turn your attention inward, away from the outer world. Notice details of your physical experience, your sensations. Is your heartbeat gentle and comfortable, or is it quick and pressured? Does your skin feel warm, cool, clammy, sweaty? Where? How cool or warm? Are your muscles tight, sore, relaxed, loose? Notice whether you feel any anxiety or tightness in your chest and stomach. What do you feel? Do you feel happy, content, sad, tired, annoyed? Link the physical components to the emotion. Do not attempt to alter your emotional state: Simply observe it in every aspect possible. Notice the experience, but try not to become lost in it; retain your vantage point of detached observer, as in previous exercises, sitting on the banks of the stream rather than being swept along with the current.

EMBRACE YOUR FEELING EXERCISE

Now that you have observed your emotions, close your eyes again for a further meditation. Sit comfortably. Allow yourself to feel the emotion fully. If you are feeling sad, let the emotion spread through you. Let it be, do not try to alter it; but if the emotional tone spontaneously changes, allow it to happen. Embrace it, accept it, be one with it. Thus, be sadness if you are sad, with no separation between you and your sadness. Do not add to it or draw conclusions. Simply allow the feeling to be, and wait.

This exercise can be especially helpful when a person is in mourning over the death of a loved one. There is a natural mourning process, somewhat like the labor of childbirth. If you endure and embrace it fully, even though it may be intensely painful, you can gain from the experience and then move forward.

CONCLUSION

Your feelings can lead you back to your natural center of balance. It does not matter whether you are happy, sad, angry, or fearful. When you accept yourself as you are, you no longer fight yourself, rejecting and judging, erratic in your energy. By embracing your feelings fully in meditation, you experience a transformation—at one with yourself, in harmony with your personality.

12
HEALING: WISDOM IS IN THE WIRING

*The human mind can discipline the body, can set
goals for itself, can somehow comprehend its own
potentiality and move resolutely forward.*

—Norman Cousins

T here are many mysteries of the body, how it can be amazingly vital. Life itself has never been duplicated. It is its own wisdom. From the beginnings of Western medicine, Hippocrates recognized the body's innate ability to heal itself. He understood that it possesses the powers to cure diseases, a *vis medicatrix naturae*. When a demand is placed upon the body, it responds by trying to reestablish balance. The body's natural ability to heal itself takes place automatically, when allowed to function.

Many of the treatments used in Western medicine work in conjunction with the body's own wisdom, *natura sanat*: Nature heals. For example, vaccinations do not kill bacteria. Instead, they inject dead or weakened viruses or bacteria that stimulate the body's immune system to develop its own resistance. Modern medicine works together with the immune system, one of the body's means of keeping us healthy.

An organism's tendency to come back into balance was researched extensively by Claude Bernard in the 1850s. Bernard took Hippocrates' understanding further. He believed that the phenomena of living beings must be considered as a harmonious whole. He recognized the interdependence of social and behavioral life. Holistic medicine follows this path. Bernard guided his peers when he said the following:

> *Physiologists and physicians must therefore always consider organisms as a whole and in detail at one and the same time, without ever losing sight of the peculiar conditions of all the special phenomena whose resultant is the individual. (Bernard 1957, 91)*

Through laboratory research Bernard saw that the *milieu interieur*, the inner environment of a living being, tends to remain stable and unchanging, even though the surrounding environment changes. He said, "It is a fixity of the *milieu interieur* which is the condition of free and independent life" (Bernard quoted in Seyle 1974, 23).

Walter B. Cannon, M.D., devoted his career as professor of physiology at Harvard Medical School between 1906 and 1942 to researching this phenomenon. He gave the name homeostasis to this natural wisdom of the body: Despite any disturbances, the body finds and maintains its own stability and balance.

> *The coordinated physiological processes which maintain most of the steady states in the organism are so complex and so peculiar to living beings—involving, as they may, the brain and nerves, the heart, lungs, kidney and spleen, all working cooperatively—that I have suggested*

*a special designation for these states, homeostasis. The
word does not imply something set and immobile, a
stagnation. It means a condition—a condition which
may vary, but which is relatively constant. (Cannon
1932, 24)*

Cannon studied and wrote in detail about the body's many defensive mechanisms that help protect us from harm and keep the body stable. As he points out in his famous book *The Wisdom of the Body* (Cannon 1932), our bodies are made of unstable materials that are very easily disturbed by even the most minute external conditions. Cannon said, "[The body's] persistence through many decades seems almost miraculous" (Cannon 1932, 20). His work explains this miracle scientifically.

Science helps us understand many mechanisms of disease and uncover very effective cures. Yet, despite the inroads that science has made in understanding disease, much remains unknown. The power of the mind, body, and spirit working in harmony is becoming recognized as an important clue to unlocking the many mysteries of the healing process, from curing a small wound to overcoming a major illness.

Eastern medicine incorporates many of these homeostatic principles in a theory of vital energy, *chi*. An invisible force that runs through the body along meridians, chi can be controlled and directed by the mind. Mind and body function together, each influencing the other. Physical phenomena can be observed and measured. These energy fluctuations are subtle and may require sensitivity along with training, to observe and assess.

The techniques of meditation presented in this chapter can be most powerful when applied in conjunction with Western medicine.

Even the Chinese, who have been practicing Eastern healing methods for centuries, found in a massive study involving thousands of subjects that the combination of Western and Eastern medicine works best (*Barefoot Doctor* 1977, v). We recommend that the techniques in this chapter be used along with conventional treatment. Find a doctor who is willing to be supportive of your efforts. More and more doctors are sympathetic to Eastern treatments, according to Norman Cousins:

> *The thousands of letters I have received from doctors*
> *have demolished any notion that physicians are univer-*
> *sally resistant to psychological, moral or spiritual factors*
> *in the healing process. (Cousins 1979, 159)*

The National Institutes of Health (NIH) has undertaken an extensive research project to study the effectiveness of alternative medicine approaches. These methods are being studied scientifically, to determine their efficacy. More and more physicians today are beginning to recognize and accept the usefulness of alternative approaches as an adjunct to traditional methods.

RESEARCH ON MIND-BODY HEALING

Researchers have become fascinated with understanding the interaction between mind and body working together for healing. More and more evidence points to meditation as the key.

Many people have been looking at the mind's potential influence on the body. Smith and McDaniel (in Rossi 1983) concluded their extensive studies of the mind's ability to influence immune-system response by saying that they felt their work established "intentional direct psychological modulation of the human immune system" (Rossi 1986, 158). They emphasized that this "modulation" is most effective when voluntary. Rossi states that "the work of Smith and his colleagues, however, implies that humans can train themselves to facilitate their own inner mind-body healing processes" (Rossi 1986, 158).

Research projects performed by psychiatrist and neurologist J. H. Schultz in the 1930s found that meditative relaxation and visualization techniques help return a diseased body to its normal homeostatic balance. He developed his own system, which he called Autogenic Therapy, and used it to cure conditions as diverse as ulcers, headaches, asthma, high blood pressure, and arthritis.

In the 1930s at the All-Union Institute of Experimental Medicine, Russian neurologist A. R. Luria performed extensive research on how visualization can be used to help control specific body processes. For example, he found that people could speed up or slow down their pulse rates depending upon whether they imagined themselves running after a train or lying in bed about to fall asleep.

Another groundbreaking physician was radiologist Carl Simonton, who utilized meditation to help cancer patients. He found that the mental state of his patients made a difference in how they responded to his radiology treatments (Simonton 1978). He came to believe that the mind can positively influence a person's immunological response.

The results of these and many other research projects provide compelling evidence that the mind can be a powerful ally in fighting disease and maintaining a higher state of wellness. The general underlying meditative principles are presented here to help you use your mind and spirit to enhance healing. The ability to focus your attention, visualize, strengthen the mind-body link, and activate the unconscious mind are all resources to be applied meditatively. When these techniques are used along with traditional medical treatment, people can improve their prognosis and handle, or at least endure, the difficulties with dignity and hope.

ALLOW HEALING

. . . be with it, keep company with it: this is the way to get rid of it.

—D. T. Suzuki

Working with any physical difficulty involves learning how to en-hance the body's built-in capacity to heal itself, reestablishing inner harmony, the natural way for the body to be.

EXPERIENCE THE BODY'S WISDOM

You can experience the wisdom of the body's abilities with this exercise. Sit or lie down comfortably. Close your eyes. Notice your breathing, in and out, as you find a natural rhythm. Notice how you do not have to do anything to bring this about, because you already know how to breathe. Con-sider your heartbeat, steady and rhythmic of itself, sending the blood pulsing through your veins and arteries, without any conscious direction from you. Your body temperature is also stable, usually neither too hot nor too cold. If external condi-tions demand it, your body adjusts, sweating to avoid becom-ing overheated, shivering to help regain some warmth. There are countless other examples of the wisdom of the body to maintain its balance within. Can you think of others?

Relaxation can help combat the disturbance to the body's natural balance brought on by illness. By allowing yourself to relax, you can help reestablish this balance and pave the way for your body to do what it knows how to do best: to heal and continue healthy living.

You can use any of the relaxation exercises offered throughout this book to help you relax your body and calm your mind. The relaxation meditation that follows is especially keyed to the body's ability to be healthy.

HEALING RELAXATION EXERCISE

Find a comfortable couch or bed and lie down on your back. If this position is not comfortable, find one that is. The body has a natural capacity to be relaxed. Everyone has experienced it spontaneously from time to time, a generalized feeling of calm and comfort. Scan through your body and notice any tension. Invite yourself to let go of any unnecessary tension and then wait for this release to take place. After a while, relax even more deeply. Allow the wisdom of your body to find its natural level of relaxation. This helps free energy for useful purposes while letting go of stressful and wasteful habitual expenditure of energy. Proper and appropriate rest is part of the healing process.

VISUALIZE HEALING

Many researchers have found that visualization can be effective in healing. If you would like to experiment with this approach, first develop your visualization skills. Review the basic meditations presented in Part Two, "Meditation Basics: The ABCs of Meditation," on picturing a color, a sound, and a memory (see pages 38 and 39). You will use these skills in the following exercises.

Many creative visualizations are possible, depending upon the ailment you are treating. We give several specific examples but encourage you to find the image that fits you and your situation.

When working with visualization to heal an illness, it is beneficial to create an image associated with the problem. You can then use this image as part of your meditation. For example, people who suffer from asthma imagine that their bronchial passages relax and open. Those with high blood pressure think about a calm and easy heartbeat. Sufferers from gastric disorders respond to a picture of their stomach or intestinal area becoming quiet, with acid leaving.

EXERCISE IN REALISTIC IMAGERY

For this type of visualization, the images should be as specific and realistic as possible. Sometimes people find it helpful to look at a textbook or a medical film on the condition to form a picture of what is happening physiologically. For example, cancer patients might picture the white blood cells engulfing and destroying the cancer cells and then carrying away the waste. Think of the mechanisms of your illness and create an image of them.

A second, less specific method can also be used. Some people find it easier to create a personal or individualized fantasy image, cartoon, or symbol. Although it might seem surprising, these indirect images can be just as effective as realistic images. They are often discovered less deliberately and more easily. The following exercise can help you discover your own creative visualization.

FANTASY IMAGE EXERCISE

Sit in your meditative position or in a comfortable chair. Close your eyes and think about the illness for a moment, but do not think of anything specific. Relax, scanning through your body, noticing what you experience in your muscles, your breathing, anything that appears in your awareness. Then ask yourself, "Could I have an interesting image occur to me to help me heal?" Let your thoughts drift as you wait for an image to appear. It may be subtle; it may even seem odd or unrelated. Try not to pass judgment. Images from the unconscious mind may seem irrational at times. Nevertheless, these images can be very helpful.

A woman who was using meditation for dental surgery pain imagined little cartoonlike characters sweeping away pain balls in her mouth. A cancer patient saw dive-bombers attacking giant bumble-bees until the menacing bees became weaker and weaker, eventually disappearing. Another imagined her immune-system cells glowing while the cancer cells became darker and darker as they died. Cancer patients and people with infections often visualize a battle of some sort, with the good guys winning, destroying the bad cells.

VISUALIZATION MEDITATION EXERCISE

After you discover your image, you are ready to begin using it. Plan to meditate at least once each day for five to fifteen minutes. It is even better if you can meditate two to three times, spread out over the day.

Go to your meditation place. You can perform this exercise either sitting or lying down, depending upon the illness. Be comfortable. Relax first, using any of the relaxation exercises described throughout this book. Then invite yourself to have the image. Picture it as vividly as possible. Sometimes people even feel something happening in their body. Give yourself time to experience the image. When you are ready to stop, open your eyes and stretch.

PROBLEM-SOLVING YOUR HEALTH

How are you preventing yourself from being healthy? If you suffer from a chronic illness, you are not the cause, but you probably do play a part. Think about your lifestyle and analyze what your part is in the equation. By improving the things that are under your control, you give your body a better opportunity to heal itself.

One way to become more healthy is to discover how you are preventing your body from finding its own healthy balance. The following exercise offers you some things to think about.

PROBLEM-SOLVING YOUR HEALTH EXERCISE

Does your diet lack certain nutrients or include foods that are unhealthy? Are you in a stressful circumstance that you want to change, but don't? Do you deprive yourself of sleep? Do you have difficulty sleeping? Or do you find yourself spending too much time lying around? Does your life include a balance between exercise and rest, quiet time and activity, work and play? Is there a relationship in your life that has problems? Is your work difficult? Do you worry a great deal? Are you chronically annoyed or fretful? Consider all aspects of your life. Look at it objectively, without passing judgment. You are beginning a positive process. If you notice something that needs improvement, think about how you could go about making a change. The future need not be the past. Meditation may help.

PAIN NEED NOT HURT YOU

We have many sensations in our lives: some pleasant, others unpleasant. Zen teaches us to deal with each sensation merely as a sensation and nothing more. All else is illusion. Pain is a sensation that can be very unpleasant, but it is still just what it is. We should not add to it; simply let it be. Our minds can intensify or lessen the sensation without our realizing it, helping us to endure suffering gracefully.

DEALING WITH PAIN

Pain can be a warning sign that something is wrong. When pain occurs, it motivates us to take the time to find out what has caused it. At other times, pain is an experience that accompanies illness and may bring with it a great deal of suffering. The modern-day solution is to take a painkiller, but meditation offers an alternative. When your doctor tells you that you are going to have some pain and offers a pill to stop it, you might like to try this exercise as an adjunct. Attitude can change how pain feels.

EXERCISE IN ALTERATION OF PAIN

Sit or lie down in a position that produces the least pain possible. Focus on the sensation of pain as a sensation and no more. Notice what it feels like. Is it hot? Pounding? Sharp? Dull? Describe it to yourself, noticing all the details, observing how it feels, locating its boundaries. Notice what feels good by comparison. Although painful, it does not have to hurt you or make you suffer. Can you accept the sensation just for what it is, noticing it but not being hurt by it? Do not let it hurt your feelings, so to speak. When you can let go of the hurt, your mind can be at peace even though you are uncomfortable. The suffering you felt will be lessened.

When you can do this, allow your body to relax. People often tighten up against pain, which makes it worse. Keep your mind and body as relaxed and calm as possible, and you will feel better. Your sensation is your awareness of the pain, not a punishment. You may have learned from early life experiences that pain is linked to punishment. Your body is not trying to punish you. Your nerves are doing their job—complaining, with good reason. Accept what is, do not resist, and the pain will be less disturbing. Be one with the pain; suffer with it, not from it.

RAISE YOUR ENERGY

Fatigue and lowered energy levels often accompany illness. Raising your energy level can help your body fight illness. Chi kung was developed by the Chinese thousands of years ago as a method to build a strong, vital, healthy body and to raise energy. It involves concentration of the mind in conjunction with gentle movements of the body to develop inner vitality, the chi. Many of these methods were developed by Buddhists to keep the monks healthy after hours of meditation. Taoists also created a great many methods for longevity and health that work with chi. When chi flows freely, you feel more alert and energetic. The following exercises are drawn from these ancient techniques to help you raise your chi, your internal energy.

MODIFIED CHI KUNG EXERCISE I

Stand with your legs shoulder-width apart and your arms hanging loosely at your sides. Close your eyes. Make fists with your hands and tighten the muscles of your arms and hands lightly. As you do this, focus all your attention on your arms and hands. Notice the sensations; feel the muscles contract. Keep all your concentration on this alone for approximately thirty seconds. Then let your hands open and relax your hands and arms. Notice how they feel longer when you release. Feel any sensations. Remain relaxed for about thirty seconds. Repeat this tightening and loosening five times, maintaining your mental focus throughout. If you feel able to, you can do it with your hands raised above your head, arms extended in front of you, or arms extended out from your sides. Follow the same pattern of tension and relaxation, focusing your attention. Eventually you will begin to feel tingling or warmth in your hands. This is your inner energy, your chi, beginning to flow.

MODIFIED CHI KUNG EXERCISE II

Once you have successfully felt your chi in your hands and arms, you can begin to experiment with circulating it. Perform Exercise I. When you feel warmth or tingling in your hands, imagine the tingling moving up your arms. Picture it moving into your shoulders. With time, you can direct it all around, especially to areas that need it for health and well-being. This exercise becomes more successful with practice and works best when you are able to maintain your mental focus.

Yogic exercises also help raise the vital force. Yoga calls this life-giving energy *prana*. The following exercise uses your visualization skills to develop your energy.

VITAL FORCE EXERCISE

This exercise can be performed lying down, with your legs and arms relaxed, with no obstructions anywhere. Close your eyes. Form a mental picture of the vital force rushing through your body. Imagine that it comes in through your nose as you inhale and then moves down into your lungs. When you exhale, send all this energy to every part of your body, to your very fingertips and toes. Repeat for several minutes. Breathe naturally, without forcing or pushing your breath. Keep a vivid picture in your mind. Perhaps the energy is like light or water. Use an image that makes sense to you. When you are finished, open your eyes and stretch.

You may also perform this exercise standing up, raising and lowering your arms, fingertips extended. There are many variations of this type of exercise, too complex for this study. Our next book will go into vital force in more detail.

Visualizations can link mind and body to help the body do what it knows how to do best: to be healthy. The meditation that follows activates the wisdom of the body.

RADIANT HEALTH EXERCISE

Sit or lie down, whichever is more comfortable. Imagine that you are very healthy, radiantly healthy. Perhaps you might recall a specific time before you were ill when you felt especially good, or maybe you would like to create an image of yourself as healthy. Whichever image you choose, visualize it as vividly as possible. Feel what you would feel if you were healthy. Notice every detail. Sometimes people like to imagine they are doing something and enjoying it. Others have found they like to imaginatively feel it without any movement. Experiment to find what works for you. Do this meditation often, daily if you are working on healing yourself. Try not to let this image ever get too far away from you.

CONCLUSION

You can learn to improve your health by proper focus of attention and concentration. Meditation can help facilitate the body's wisdom to do what it already knows how to do, by engaging the mind, body, and spirit.

13
STRESS: TO SHOOT
AN ARROW,
FIRST BEND THE BOW

What is the meaning
Of this moment in time?
How can I stop stopping
The flow of this mind?

—C. Alexander Simpkins

WHAT IS STRESS?

S tress seems to be all around us. From the moment we are startled by the alarm clock's harsh ring in the morning to the last bit of activity before we close our eyes at night, our lives are filled with demands, delays, and deadlines. Yet, rather than avoiding such things, we often find ourselves taking on more of them. What is stress, this all-too-common experience that plagues and entices us? And how can we best deal with it?

EARLY CONCEPTS OF STRESS

The word "stress" is very old. In Middle English "stresse" meant hardship, and in Old French "destresse" referred to constraint. Physics took the word out of the realm of human experience and into the scientific arena in the 1700s, defining it as the force or pressure exerted on a material object. By the nineteenth century, physics' concept of stress became a very specific principle of elasticity, with its own equation.

Gradually the idea of stress found its way back to people. Sir William Osler, the famous early twentieth-century physician, equated stress and strain with hard work and worry. He said that every physician he knew suffered from it because of "the incessant treadmill of the practice of medicine, and in every one of these men there was an added factor—worry" (Hinkle 1977, 30).

STRESS SYNDROME

Hans Selye popularized the concept of stress as a distinct nonspecific syndrome of its own, separate from disease and illness. He thought of this idea somewhat by accident. As a medical student in 1926, Selye noticed that although the patients he studied had different diseases, they all seemed to share certain common symptoms, like tiredness and loss of appetite. It was not until the 1950s that Selye's research led him back to his early conclusion that there is an actual syndrome which he called stress. Stress, he firmly believed, was a nonspecific reaction of the body to any demand that is placed upon it.

Harold G. Wolff, a contemporary of Selye, invented the concept of "life stress." He believed stress was the result of people's interaction with harmful agents or circumstances. For Wolff, Selye, and other researchers of this period, stress was an actual "state" that took place in the body.

STRESS CAN BE GOOD FOR YOU!

These early theories of stress did not continue to bear out. Researchers did not find a correlation between hardships and the appearance of disease. World War II showed both the expected results of exposure to trauma and cases of the unexpected opposite. At times, soldiers and concentration camp survivors lost their illnesses such as ulcers, migraines, and colitis—diseases that had previously been thought to be caused by stress. This made it necessary to revise the stress concept.

Researchers found that people need a certain amount of stress for optimum functioning. John C. Whitehorn M.D., director of Phipps Clinic at Johns Hopkins University Hospital, wrote an article titled "The Healthful Benefits of Stress" (Whitehorn 1956, 646). He pointed out that without challenge and meaningful involvement, "purposeful personal striving" (Whitehorn 1956, 647), people become unhappy and often ill.

Thus, stress is not to be avoided; sometimes it should be embraced. A recent news brief from Birmingham, England, reported that experiments have shown that playing computer games can briefly lift people's immune system. "The immune system is constantly fluctuating . . . it is constantly going up and down, and what it is trying to do is maintain a balance," according to Phil Evans M.D. He went on to say, "It is important to put a brake on people who say that stress constantly down-regulates the system" (Reuter News Summary, America Online, September 9, 1996).

HOW WE HANDLE STRESS CAN HELP

How we cope with stress can have a profound effect on how stress effects us. Barbara Snell Dohrenwend and Bruce P. Dohrenwend (1981) noted in their extensive research that some people become ill when exposed to life stress but others do not. They wondered why. They discovered that the mind plays a large part in how stress affects people. Expectations about the stressfulness of an event can influence the effects of stress. When a situation is appraised as a challenge rather than a threat, people cope better.

Irving Janis found that coping well is due to accurate perception (1971, 97). He followed the outcome of patients undergoing major surgery and found that people coped well when they had realistic expectations. People who clearly perceive the truth about the stressor cope better, thereby lessening the harmful effects of severe stress.

Richard Lazarus pointed out that cognitive appraisals, that is, what people think about stressful situations, can have an effect on the outcome (Lazarus 1977, 14). Sometimes an attitude of detachment helps people manage a difficult situation (such as a serious loss of function from illness) until they can emotionally handle the knowledge about what they must inevitably live with. Visualization of positive changes in the body can also reverse psychological or physical processes, by encouraging hope and faith in the mysteries of the body. There is a great deal that is not known, and it is likely that much more is possible than people would imagine.

What seems to be a mediating variable is how people interpret and handle the stressors in their lives. Our interpretations and the meaning we give to circumstances, our physical predispositions, and life situation all affect how we handle stress. Stress is a complex concept, with many factors at work. The NIH initiated a $10 million project, still in progress, to find out what these factors are.

The many studies on stress have led researchers to admit that the mind plays a predominant role in stress management. What better way, then, to deal with stress in your life than through the age-old wisdom of meditation?

COPING WITH STRESS

Based upon the research that has been done on stress, there are ways you can learn to cope better by using meditation. When your life presents you with difficult situations, you can handle them with less harmful stress. The body's own mechanisms of defense against stress help you regain homeostasis. You can use your mind to achieve inner balance and function optimally. Below are some helpful exercises drawn from the wisdom of meditation.

RELAXATION: INNER CALM

Life without stress is impossible. Life calls upon us to take on challenges, sometimes by choice, other times by chance. When circumstances push us to our limit, we may lose our center in the effort to keep up. The body cries out for rest, yet the opportunity may not be available. Meditation draws on the inner mind to find calm amid the storm, just enough rest to allow us to carry on. These exercises develop skills in relaxation, first of the body, then of the mind. You can use these intermittently in your day to help allay the negative effects of an overly demanding schedule. The following two exercises, drawn from Yoga, are designed to help you relax the tensions that stress can bring.

BODY RELAXATION

Lie on your back, with your knees drawn up and feet flat on the floor. You may want to add a small, thin cushion under your lower back to relieve tension. This position offers comfort to the back muscles, which often become tense when the body is stressed. A variation of this position is to lie on your side on the floor or on a soft rug, with your head on a pillow, legs bent, knees pulled in. Again, a thin pillow under your hips or shoulders may help align your body comfortably. Close your eyes and allow your breathing to be relaxed. Imagine, with every breath out, that tensions in your muscles ease. If you notice any particularly tight area, try to let go using your breathing. Rest comfortably for five minutes or so, breathing out tightness. When you feel ready, sit up and stretch.

RELAXATION USING SYMBOLS

Close your eyes. Sit comfortably, in one of the usual positions. Imagine that you are sitting by a flowing stream. You watch from the bank. Despite the many twigs and leaves that drift along in the stream, there is always the stream, ever flowing, always there, carrying the twigs and leaves along. The twigs and leaves represent thoughts, feelings, memories, and plans. Stay with the stream, observing. You might notice an interesting branch as it floats by, but do not be swept along with it. Always the deeper flow of the stream is there, flowing onward. Keep your attention fully focused on the stream. As with the stream, so with your mind—clear, ever flowing.

A young professional in therapy had an image of himself as a lumberjack standing by a stream, directing logs downward. He saw himself on the shore downstream, feeling out of control as he watched the logs rush toward a narrow point in the stream. There, they jammed together, unable to continue the flow of their journey. He felt helpless to do anything about it, just as he felt with the many problems in his life. We suggested that, using meditative trance, he try to walk upstream, to direct the logs before they began to jam, guiding them into the appropriate channels, ensuring that they were correctly spaced apart and flowing with the currents of the stream. After he was able to do this meditatively, he found that he was dealing with his actual life situations before they became problems. His stress eased, and he coped better with the demands of his life.

You can experiment with images in meditation that have personal symbolic significance. Often these visualizations occur spontaneously. The insights gained in meditation filter into your everyday actions.

JUST DO IT

Stress can be increased when we do not adequately meet our circumstances. Sometimes the demands of a job may seem so great that people back off, changing a challenge into a stressful situation. Zen Buddhism teaches you to approach each task wholeheartedly and just do it. There is no wavering, no conceptual evaluations, no "should I" or "shouldn't I," only ardent effort, with mind, body, and spirit working together as one.

The enlightened Zen Buddhist is not troubled by many of the things that bother the everyday individual, including stress. Zen monks make meditation a part of every activity throughout the day, including their work, meals, and rest. Novices always wonder, How can

I bring mindfulness of meditation into my daily life? An analogy may help.

Think of a time when you were very thirsty but were unable to get a drink of water. Perhaps you were in the car on a long drive, and you were running late. You tried to put your thirst out of your mind but could not. The more you attempted to put it out of your mind, the thirstier you felt. Eventually your mind was so entirely filled with thirst that you pulled off the road at the next restaurant to get some water.

With the same persistent intensity as your unsatisfied thirst, focus on your here-and-now experience in your life. Stay with it when you are walking, dressing in the morning, eating meals, spending time with your family, doing your work. Gradually your mind clears and you find yourself just doing what you are doing. Any worries and problems drop away. What remains is just you and your task, whatever it is. You are completely immersed in it, and there is no separation.

Ma-tsu taught Zen during its most creative period, the T'ang dynasty. He expressed this way of living when he said, "When hungry I eat, when tired I sleep" (Suzuki 1969, 106). A student questioned a Zen master further about Ma-tsu's statement, asking how this way of simply eating and sleeping was so different. The master answered as follows:

> *When they eat, they do not just eat, they conjure up all kinds of imagination; when they sleep, they do not just sleep, they are given up to varieties of idle thoughts, that is why theirs is not my way. (Suzuki 1969, 106)*

For people today, the Zen meditative path can be helpful in dealing with stress. You can lose yourself in your daily routines, doing them with such full attention that nothing distracts or disturbs you. Then what happens to your stress?

MINDFULNESS EXERCISE FOR STRESS

Think about a situation you are trying to master. It could be related to your job or your home life. Review carefully what it is you need to do. Visualize it as clearly as possible. Keep your mind on the situation itself, as you address it moment to moment. Pressures from time, other people, and goals are secondary, outside the circle of your focus. When you remain fully present in the situation that you are finding stressful, you may discover that your worries take on less importance and even become background.

LETTING BE

If stress mounts as you try harder and harder, expending more and more energy to accomplish less and less, you may need to take a Taoist approach. There are times when we must be flexible enough to back off, to yield to circumstance. Taoism's solution is radically different from Zen: *wu-wei*, or the way of nonaction. What seems difficult becomes easy and flows naturally. Sometimes the things we do effortlessly turn out the best. The next exercise guides you in applying this principle to your work.

Do by not doing, act by non-action, taste the taste-
    less, regard small as great, much as little
Plan what is difficult where it is easy; Do what is
    great where it is minute.
The hardest things in the world begin with what is
    easy; the greatest things in the world begin with
    what is minute.
        —*Tao te Ching,* chapter 63, translated by J. J. L. Duyvendak

NONACTION MEDITATION

The outer comes from the inner, the mind. This meditation begins a process of nonaction through letting be. Sit quietly. Close your eyes. Do you permit your eyes to rest, or are they watching? Notice this but do not change it. Pay attention to your breathing, but do not alter it. Simply allow it to be as it is. Scan through your body. Notice any tension, but do not try to make yourself relax. Allow your muscles to be as they are. How does your body meet the floor? Do you let the floor support your body, or are you holding yourself off the floor? Notice these things. Now turn your attention to your thoughts. Note any thoughts that occur to you, but do not attempt to direct them. Simply observe, allowing them to be as they are. Follow whatever your awareness presents to you, but do not try to change. Be as you are. After sustaining this for up to fifteen minutes, notice your experience. Did your breathing become easier? Did your muscles relax of their own accord? Do you feel calmer? In noticing, without altering anything purposefully, a change begins to take place of itself. Allow your organism to find its natural balance.

When you pause to reflect on things as they are, without altering anything on purpose, something emerges. With time, your natural rhythms begin to reassert themselves. Chuang-tzu taught his students to overcome their difficulties by permitting nature to take its course. Let nature take its course, and it will guide you well. To become one with nature is to trust our nature within. As we begin to listen to our bodies, the rhythms of appetite, fatigue, and energy can guide us.

STRESS AND TIME

People often feel that they do not have enough time. Westerners are goal oriented, filling every minute with plans and activities. Internal conversations echo, "I have to go here; I've got to do that." Plans and goals are important and useful, but allowing some unplanned time to simply be can help keep the busy person in balance, as you may have discovered in the previous exercise. This ancient fable illustrates the point:

> God sent an angel to earth to offer eternal life in ex-
> change for a moment of human time. But the angel
> had to return to God without delivering the gift be-
> cause, when he reached earth, he discovered that ev-
> eryone was living with one foot in the past and one
> foot in the future. No one had a moment of time.
> (Keene 1979, 70)

A MEDITATIVE MOMENT

Meditation draws on the inner recesses of the mind, a timeless space of experience that does not rely on the ticking of a clock. We have all felt this—for example, when a few minutes during a boring meeting or class seems like an hour, or conversely, when a whole day of vacation seems to pass like a flash. This quality of the inner mind allows regular, short meditative breaks to have long-lasting effects. This exercise can be done almost anytime: at your desk at the office, in the evening just before sleep, during your child's nap, or as part of your coffee break. Making this exercise, and many of the exercises included in this book, part of your daily routine can set the stage for a less harried, calmer life.

MEDITATIVE RETREAT EXERCISE

Find a comfortable position, either seated or lying down. Close your eyes. Breathe normally, comfortably. Let go of any unnecessary tension. Recall a place or a time when you felt very relaxed and calm. Perhaps you were on vacation, with a good friend or loved one, or perhaps you were alone. Vividly imagine yourself there once again. Remember how you felt, what things looked like, any memorable smells or tastes: every possible detail you can recall. As you fill your mind with this relaxing memory, you may find your body spontaneously relaxing. Allow this to take place naturally. When you feel ready, open your eyes and return to the present moment, relaxed and refreshed.

BALANCE

You can discover harmony within so that your life flows more smoothly. Each of us has an optimal balance point. Some people function at a very high energy level. As one of our clients once told us, she did not feel comfortable unless she was "off tilt." Other people like to live a quieter, slower-paced life. There are times in life when even the quietest person is called upon to put forth an extra effort. Sometimes we choose to meet a challenge. Learning to recognize your own rhythms, when to push and when to withdraw, allows you to accomplish more naturally and comfortably, without stress. There is a unique adjustment point that is optimal for each person. Meditation can help you find your own balance.

14
ATHLETICS:
WHEN YOU ARE ONE,
YOU HAVE WON

See first with the mind, then with the eyes, and
finally with the body and limbs.

—Yagyu, Japanese swordsman

S piritual fitness is a new form of exercise and sports that has emerged in recent years, combining Eastern practices and mind-body awareness. Programs at health-club facilities, in universities, and at recreation centers in major cities offer experimental programs in mind-body sports. The focus is different from that in traditional sports. Integrating meditation and sport can be the springboard to well-being in mind and body.

Participants learn how to concentrate on their training, to actually meditate while working out. Spiritual athletes achieve distinct benefits for health, morale, and relief of stress. They get fewer injuries and find more fulfillment than they would in traditional sports. Exercise that enhances the mind-body connection requires more intellectual effort, but as one student said, "Aerobics was boring. This stimulates me intellectually." Chi kung stretch classes

To what heights may
you not ascend?

and meditative aerobics are some of the new spiritual athletics available.

Martial arts have been combining exercise with meditation for centuries. "Karate is Zen and Zen is Karate," the famous martial artist Mas Oyama once said (Oyama 1979, 67). Martial arts are the epitome of meditative action. Participation involves unwavering focus on movement. This capacity to focus attention is enhanced by intensity. Strong emotional arousal tends to heighten attention by activating the part of the brain that controls this kind of functioning, the reticular activating system at the base of the brain. The internal energy (chi) is raised, so that each movement is performed with full focus of mind, body, and spirit working together as one.

For decades, champion bodybuilders have extolled the virtues of using mental exercises when lifting heavy weights. They believe that power and muscle development is greatly assisted by the mind. While working out with specific exercises, such as bench press and arm curls, they visualize their muscles contracting, getting pumped up with blood, and growing larger and stronger. Tom Platz, a renowned bodybuilder, had a saying: "Whatever can be conceived can be believed; whatever can be believed can be achieved." Arnold Schwarzenegger, seven-time undefeated Mr. Olympia champion, visualized his biceps as mountains, growing in size as he trained. He felt that visualization helped his arms become one of his greatest assets in bodybuilding.

You can incorporate meditation directly into your own exercise regimen, whether your workouts include individual activities like weightlifting, running, aerobics, tennis or martial arts or team sports such as soccer, baseball, or basketball. The exercises in this chapter help you to focus inwardly.

THE MIDDLE WAY

Many coaches, athletes, and exercise physiologists recognize how important rest and recovery are for optimum performance. The correct balance of rest can actually improve physical fitness. Long-distance swimmer Lynne Cox, who has had more than thirty-five international swims (including the English Channel) found that overambitious training without a corresponding recuperative cycle actually prevented her from succeeding in her Catalina Channel swim! After a two-week rest, she attempted the swim again and broke the record.

Too little exercise, the opposite extreme, is also unhealthy. The National Aeronautics and Space Administration learned of the negative effects of prolonged rest. Astronauts who underwent weightlessness in space returned home from missions less fit than when they left. Muscles and bones deteriorated and blood pressure dropped. The same problem confronts people who are bedridden. NASA found that even brief periods of exercise could turn this degeneration around.

The best way to stay fit and healthy lies somewhere between the two extremes. Joe Houmard, an associate professor at the Human Performance Laboratory at East Carolina University said, "You have athletes who don't want to stop for anything. That's one end of the spectrum. Then you have people who will stop for any reason. The best is the middle" (Zimmer 1996, 5). People who meditate have long recognized the wisdom of the middle way. The middle is different for each individual. The following exercise may help you find your balance.

CONTEMPLATE YOUR TRAINING

With the middle way in mind, contemplate your own athletic training. Think of a typical week. Do you train until you are sore? Or are you barely training? Do you allow time for your muscles to recover? A cycle of training and rest is optimal, but must be individualized. Imagine what would be a balance for you, taking into account your capacities, goals, and level of commitment.

BODY AWARENESS IN SPACE

The thing is not to try to localize the mind anywhere
but to let it fill up the whole body, let it flow
throughout the totality of your being. When this
happens you use the hands when they are needed,
you use the legs or the eyes when they are needed,
and no time or no extra energy will be wasted.

—Takuan, Zen master

Spatial body awareness is very important in many sports. Not only must you be aware of your own muscles and balance; you also need to develop a felt sense of your body in an environmental or spatial context. It might be in relation to a court, a field, or even another player. Meditation can heighten your awareness of how you interrelate with objects in space.

MOVEMENT CONTEMPLATION EXERCISE

With awareness, slowly concentrate on every movement as you clear the table or set the table. Be aware of breathing, of walking, of the weight and temperature of the plates and dishes. Let go of the need for an exact purpose or a deadline, yet be efficient with motion, graceful, and balanced in movement. Many variations are possible.

Take this same contemplative frame of mind to your sport. For example, if you are a tennis player, pick up your racket and notice its weight, shape, textures. Swing it slowly and feel your body in relation to the racket. Notice yourself in position on the court. Move closer to the net, then farther back: sense your relationship to the net. Pay attention to changes in perspective and your body experience. Just play and enjoy!

For soccer players, perform this awareness exercise with the ball as you toss it in the air, then roll it over your arm. Be creative, always maintaining mental concentration. Move around on the court (or the field) and notice your body experience from different places and in relation to your opponent as well. Whatever your sport, you can experience your interrelationship to the environment by focusing your attention on it.

SEEK PERFECTION, PERMIT IMPERFECTION EXERCISE

What is your aesthetic experience of motion before you think about it? Can you enjoy it just for what it is as you do it? Can you feel the action of running or taking a walk, just as that, with no purpose? Children do this sometimes, breaking into a run simply for the joy of movement. What do you notice? Can you be graceful without effort?

Now, after you have run or walked awhile, find a place to meditate quietly. Relax. Allow yourself to reexperience the run or walk, feeling it from within. Then return home, keeping this state of being, this spirit of awareness. Movement for no purpose, just to run or walk, may be difficult for us to justify, yet it is necessary.

OVERCOMING LIMITS: WINNING MIND

The concept or image that you have of yourself, including your potential and capacity, tends to stabilize and guide you and your behavior, but it can also limit you. When you want to achieve excellence, to break a record, or to win a difficult game, you must be willing to be uncertain of what your limit really is. Your concept is not your true capacity. You must do what you can at the time, without any thought of the outcome. Outcome is afterward, to ratify what has transpired. Immerse yourself in the process of the moment. You can best address this by setting aside concepts and simply being there.

JUST LISTENING EXERCISE

One of the most absorbing things to listen to is your own voice as you talk to others. Do not pay attention to content, to what you say. Instead, notice how you sound. Can you listen without value judgment, without praise or condemnation, without comparison? Try recording and playing back a conversation. Can you just listen? Listen to the echo, to the tone, the pauses between words, the rhythms.

Apply this same frame of mind while performing your sport. Notice the movement, the rhythms, your breathing, your muscles, but do not pass judgment. Keep the meditative awareness with you throughout.

In sports, the willingness within, the will to win, is a vital variable. Players must give themselves fully to the moment of action, doing what needs to be done. Here, meditation reminds us of its timeless message of Oneness. Willingness to win is part of this unity: mind, body, and spirit must function together in action as one. When they do not, achievement suffers. In Oneness with action, the impossible becomes possible.

The willingness to fully immerse yourself in the effort without regard for negative consequences or for losing is an important part of sports performance. There is an element of loss in every gain, according to Taoism.

Consider what there is to lose (or to win) before the game. Sometimes it is actually more threatening to win than to lose! We might rationally think that winning is an obvious plus, but to win, to succeed, might bring other consequences in its wake. You may need to confront, accept, and contemplate these issues as you accept your feelings. If it really is possible for you to win, then perhaps other successes are possible, too; paradoxically, that may be threatening to your security and comfort. Perhaps you have a stable, comfortable life based on keeping the status quo. You know how to make yourself happy, you know yourself and your limits. But from the opposite perspective, you may find a new image of your possibilities to be exciting, exhilarating. Perhaps your limits may not be a wall, a barrier, but seen from a different perspective, a springboard. To risk this is worthwhile but may require a new attitude.

To win or to lose is not two different things; concern with winning or losing is a distraction except insofar as it may motivate some people to take the steps necessary to make the effort. But the moment of effort must transcend concern for winning and losing: it must just be. The great kicker does not kick the ball between the goal posts to win the game, he kicks the ball exactly between the goal posts, and thereby wins the game. The world-class runner does not run faster to win the race, she simply moves quicker to run faster and thus wins the race.

Sports are one more way that we can learn to set aside superficial mental constructs to be more fully our best. In the moment of doing, you just do!

NEW ATTITUDE EXERCISE

Next time you play a game or go to practice, set aside all thoughts of winning or losing. Instead, perform each play with full effort. Do not think about the outcome, do not concern yourself about the past. Simply play: run, swim, golf, whatever the sport, staying focused in the moment, meditatively present. Suspend concepts. Set aside the game's goal. Search within and you will win!

TEAM UNITY

In team sports, the individual athlete attempts to be part of the total play, to seek the goal of the game and the team rather than a self-oriented one. This aim overlaps with meditation. Eastern philosophies believe that each individual is always part of the greater whole. In Taoism, for example, by becoming one with the Tao, the one takes on the attributes of the whole and is in tune with the nature of things. Everything flows more naturally, comes easier. Chuang-tzu said, "If one observes the Way of Heaven and maintains Its doings (as his own) all that he has to do is accomplished" (Legge 1962, 257).

Giving yourself to the sport not only with a time commitment but also in spirit and emotion is what it is all about. The team effort—getting one's own ego unified with the other team members—is vital. Coaches believe players learn important lessons about life through this team effort. Meditation brings more depth to the sports experience.

Willingness to win is an aspect of team Oneness. This exercise can help both you as an individual and an entire team meditating together to rediscover team unity.

Meditation as a team.
Iae Chun Do Martial Arts students meditate together, as one.

OVERCOMING BLOCKS
TO TEAM ONENESS EXERCISE

Clinging to previous concepts of yourself as not a winner or to the past history of the team affects the moment of facing ultimate tests. How do your team and the individual members confront their history? When a team consistently loses year after year, it may not be because of individual players but often involves something deeper that affects performance of the team as a whole. What meaning does it take on? Is the past a source of inspiration or of disconfirmation? Can you be in the present rather than in the past?

Can you approach the next game, the next half of play, the next point, as if it were the first, the beginning? Practice clearing your mind in meditation. Then bring this mind-set to the next game.

MEDITATION AS A TEAM

Meditating together can help a team reclaim lost unity or strengthen the Oneness that is there. Sit down on the floor in a circle. Quietly experience a few minutes together, without any speaking. Simply be together, as a team, quietly, regularly. Sometimes you may want to close your eyes. At other sessions, keep your eyes open. With time, group meditation can help bring about stronger bonds among team members.

Mount Fuji
"If this snail sets out for the top of
Fuji, surely he will get there."
—Tesshu, Japanese swordsman
Japanese, twentieth century scroll.
Ink on paper.
Bequest of Elsie S. Kimberly.
San Diego Museum of Art.

15

WORK AND RELATIONSHIP: EARNING EDEN

The student goes to school, the army serves the country, and the teacher works for all students. The dog is barking, "Woof, woof," the rooster is crowing, "Cock-a-doodle-doo!" Each one understands its job. What is your job?

—Seung Sahn, Korean Zen master

Meditation does not necessarily require you to isolate yourself, withdrawing alone into a quiet room for calmness. Activity, excitement, work, relationship—all can be opportunities to meditate and transcend the dualities and the limitations of worldly existence, yet remain fully there, fully present and in touch. Success and accomplishment are not excluded, nor should they be.

The current president of Mozambique, Joaquim Chissano, holds one of the most challenging jobs imaginable. He has seen his country through revolution, civil war, and drought. He attributes his ability to face the formidable responsibilities of his job to daily meditation. He has been meditating for several years; now his wife meditates, his sons meditate, as do his cabinet, most of his generals, and even the Mozambique military! When asked what meditation has done for him, he answered as follows:

It is like recharging your batteries. One tends to feel the same effects as someone who has had a long rest, only in a shorter period. But the most important effect of meditation for me is to control my stress. Meditation changes the way you face difficult problems! (Roach, 1995)

He credits meditation with giving him the inner strength and calmness to rule wisely. No matter what type of work you do, meditation can help you work more efficiently and with less stress.

THE IMPORTANCE OF WORK

Zen Buddhism has long understood the importance of work. Early on in the development of Zen, work was incorporated into the daily schedule. This was a distinct change from traditional Buddhism in India, where itinerant monks wandered with only a begging bowl and the robes on their back. They never worked and were completely dependent upon others for their sustenance.

Pai-chang, a Chinese monk (720–814), first instituted the monastic system still followed today. Work was performed by all monks as an essential element of the daily routine. An ancient story shows how seriously Pai-chang took his work on the farm. When he was very elderly, his devoted monks decided to spare their master from his daily toil in the fields. Benevolently, they hid his gardening tools and told him, "Master, now you may have a rest from your duties."

Much to their surprise, Pai-chang's response was not gratitude. Instead, he refused to eat, saying, "A day without work is a day without food." The monks were forced to give up their plan, and they returned his tools to him. People dedicated to meditation bring their meditation with them into their work, so that spirituality fills every corner of their lives.

The statement "A day of no work is a day of no eating" is the literal translation of the first rule for monastic life. As D.T. Suzuki stated:

> But as long as this meditation remains identified
> with abstractions, there will be no practical solu-
> tions to the problems. . . . Zen masters have there-
> fore been anxious to see their monks work hard on
> the farm, in the woods, or in the mountains. (Suzuki
> 1994, 33–34)

There are numerous stories of Zen monks working at all sorts of labors. They found deep meaning in everything they did. One time Chao-chou, a famous monk from the T'ang period in China, was hard at work sweeping around the monastery. A young monk saw his esteemed master engaged in sweeping and felt puzzled that he should do such lowly work. He asked, "You are an enlightened Zen monk, free from the dust of evil thoughts, so why do you need to sweep?"

The master immediately answered, "The dust comes from outside!" The monks made no dualistic distinctions between thought and action. All thoughts, all actions, offer an opportunity for growth and learning. Work is sacred.

FINDING YOUR PLACE: CAREER GUIDANCE

There are many successful behavioral methods to help people find what type of work suits them. These approaches offer a complete career-planning guide that can be very useful in matching the person to the career. People learn more about themselves, discovering what type of person they are. Then they match their personality traits with the traits required by various jobs and professions. Eastern wisdom offers a uniquely different approach. Readers may wish to combine the Western and Eastern methods.

According to Eastern thought, the path that people choose for a career is not based on their sense of self but rather evolves as they get attuned to the Way. The qualities of personal self are not central. Take the correct path, seek the Way, and you will find yourself.

From this perspective, the search for a career involves blending of the self with the nature of the particular career. When there is harmony, things flow effortlessly. We have all met people who are at one with their careers. They are at ease with the work, seem to "look the part," and find great personal satisfaction in doing what they do. This exercise can help you discover your path.

BE ONE WITH YOUR WORK EXERCISE

Think about the profession you are considering. Visualize the Way of this career. All jobs pay money, of course, but look beyond the monetary benefits. What is the nature of this work? For example, psychologists, social workers, counselors, and doctors are helpers. Architects and engineers affect the environment. Restaurant managers, chefs, and waitresses serve and nourish others. Businesspeople provide things for others at a profit. You will have your own interpretations and definitions. Consider the essence of your career choice. On a fundamental personal level, can you imagine yourself walking this path? Visualize yourself in this career. Picture yourself going to work and doing the job. Would you be able to be in harmony with this Way, and in doing the work, to continue in harmony with the Way?

MASTERY

Buddhism believes that work is not only a job to be done but a manifestation of the miracle of being alive. "Right livelihood" is part of Buddha's prescribed Eightfold Path. He believed that to be happy, people must develop their skills and be efficient, earnest, energetic, and sincere in whatever their profession or job may be.

Mindfulness is the method that Buddhism offers to accomplish this: staying relaxed, alert, with your mind clear and focused. You can experiment with this form of meditation using a small, time-limited task. Eventually you can bring the skills you develop here into your daily lifework.

MINDFULNESS MEDITATION EXERCISE

Pick a small task, such as doing the laundry or washing the windows. Before you begin, concentrate on what you are about to do. Gather the things you need to accomplish this job. Set them out carefully where you plan to do the work. Sit for a moment and clear your mind. Focus your attention on your present experiencing. Look around you and notice yourself in your surroundings. When you feel gathered and ready, begin the task. Keep your attention focused on exactly what you are doing and nothing else. If you become distracted, bring your attention back to the task, just as you have done in previous meditations. Work silently, that is, do not talk to anyone else unless it is necessary, and do not carry on any inward dialogue with yourself. Put all your energy into doing your best on this task and only this task. Do not jump ahead, anticipating how it will look when it is done or thinking about what you might have planned for later. When you are finished, carefully put away everything that you brought out, mindful throughout

Mindfulness Meditation Exercise, continued

the process. "Leave no trace," as the Buddhists say, so that everything is as it was before you began, except for the clean clothes in the closet or the sparkling clear windows, and your clear mind.

The Taoists also understood how we can find inner peace and fulfillment through our work. Taoists seek to live and be at one with the Tao. The Tao is everywhere and in everything. Complete immersion in action brings a person closer to the Tao. By being one with your occupation, whatever it is, you will eventually become a master.

There is no room for anxious thoughts, doubts, or worries with this orientation toward work. In time, skills develop that carry you to new possibilities. Work offers the opportunity to realize your potential. You evolve through your occupation, whatever it is, finding harmony and balance with yourself and your world. The key is wholehearted and full participation.

> *Life exacts a price for less than full participation.*
> *We lose touch with the human values and qualities*
> *that spring naturally from a full engagement with*
> *work and life: integrity, honesty, loyalty, responsibil-*
> *ity, and cooperation. (Whitmyer 1994, 29)*

MEDITATION EXERCISE ON LIFEWORK

Approach a task at your job using mindful meditation. Pick something that is time-limited or is one small part of a larger project. Before beginning, prepare as you did in the previous exercise, gathering what you need. If your job involves mental work, ready your mind. If you need to prepare some materials, do so. If your work is physical, warm up your body. Take a few minutes to clear your mind; meditate deeply. When you feel ready, begin the task energetically. Put your full attention on it; concentrate on your performance. For example, if you are typing, allow your fingers to move smoothly and quickly over the keys. If you are doing labor, let the stroke of your tools be sure and true. Strive for exact, efficient action with each motion of the tool. Keep your body relaxed, yet adequately attuned to what your work requires, and empty your mind of extraneous thoughts as you stay focused on the material, free of distraction. Do not deviate. When you are finished and feel that you have done the job thoroughly, meditate for a minute or two. Now put away everything you used. Leave no trace. As you do this, keep your attention focused on these actions; do not jump ahead to what comes next, except as needed.

MEDITATION WITH DISTRACTIONS

Meditation can teach you to clear your mind and stay steadfast despite adverse circumstances. In this exercise, perform a clearing-the-mind meditation. However, instead of meditating in a quiet place without interruptions, pick a place where you will be distracted. It is probably best to begin at home, perhaps with the television or radio playing. Start with a very short meditation (two minutes) and work your way up to twenty minutes.

MEDITATION AND RELATIONSHIPS

We are part of one another
We are aware
Without one standard
By which to compare
In the Mysterious Oneness
Of the Universe
None is better, none is worse.
—C. Alexander Simpkins

Mindfulness and awareness extend into all aspects of life. Meditation may seem like a solitary endeavor that takes you further inside yourself. Paradoxically, meditation takes you deeper into yourself to find a more profound, more compassionate nature that takes you beyond yourself and into the realm of relationship to others. Your interpersonal relationships, both in the workplace and in your personal life, can be improved with meditation.

SOCIAL AWARENESS

Certain forms of meditation aim directly to guide people in their relationships with the world. Benevolence and compassion are part of the tradition of meditation. Anyone willing to adopt this attitude will find greater balance in career and relationship. It is possible to be sincerely committed to meditation and still be deeply involved in the world.

Unselfish actions and behavior can help eradicate or resolve tensions from imbalances, whether from within your own personality or from other aspects of your life. Acting, doing something, especially with regard to others, can help you break out of this circle. "Empathy and understanding are facts of social feeling, of harmony with the universe" (Adler 1959, 41).

It is almost impossible to exaggerate the value of increased social feeling to mental well-being. Your feeling of worth and value is heightened, giving you self-confidence and an optimistic view.

Social feeling implies including and integrating oneself within the larger whole of society and ultimately the universe. We can sense this larger unity around us through our experience. Many problems can improve through Oneness in relationship.

ONENESS IN RELATIONSHIP

Self-absorption is a fundamental aspect of problematic adjustments to life. Meditation offers an attitude of self-surrender, in which you learn to let go of negative self-centeredness. This letting go affects relationships positively, but it must be mutual to work. If one surrenders his or her self-interest while the other does not, an imbalance is created that precludes mutual satisfaction. The true nature of a relationship inevitably asserts itself as the relationship evolves to completion. When both parties are wholeheartedly willing, nature takes its course and things work out. The natural way is harmonious.

Excessive emotion is not conducive to peacefulness. Meditation can help people gain the calm to address issues with objectivity. A problem-solving attitude helps bring this about. Feelings and perceptions have to be aired sincerely; but without facing what needs to be altered or accomplished (and then doing it), no solution is possible.

You can handle anger through calm with positive results. There are appropriate times to release anger, but there are other times when being calm is better. Calmness need not imply that you are passive and ignore problems or that you become frustrated and pressured. Calming is brought about when difficulties are addressed and resolution is sought. Correctly using your feelings can lead to being more attuned and satisfied.

INTERPERSONAL ANGER RESOLUTION

Next time you are feeling angry with someone, take a meditation break. Pause for a moment to gather yourself, and take a few minutes to meditate. If you are accustomed to meditation, you can do this very quickly. Feel your body, the tightness in your stomach, chest, or wherever you feel this emotion. Can you let go a bit? Think about the difficulty, your annoyance. Consider what the other person is feeling. Can you imagine how that person feels from his or her own point of view? Your own view may differ, but can you accept the validity of the other's perspective? As you contemplate these things, think about your relationship, the greater whole. Breathe comfortably and try to relax your tension a little more. Seek your center. When you feel calmer overall, open your eyes. Can you work out the difficulties now?

Conflicts between friends and within relationships can sometimes be resolved more simply than might be imagined, but such resolution needs to be within the relationship: Oneness is a potential, not an actuality.

NO COMPARISON

Better to see the face than to hear the name.
—Zen saying

When working or living in a situation with others, people sometimes feel as though they are at a disadvantage. The other person seems to have an easier time, even to be given preferential treatment. People often think in terms of rankings: this one is higher than that one. For the Buddhist, such concerns are considered invalid. There are no comparisons. No one thing or person is better than another. Lin-chi, founder of the famous Rinzai sect of Zen, created the idea of the person of no rank who was the truly enlightened one. He stated: "He is without form, without characteristics, without root, without source, without any dwelling place, yet is brisk and lively" (quoted in Dumoulin 1988, 193). Understanding this does not come from the praise of others, from prizes or promotions. The real source is from within.

All people have the potential to overcome trying circumstances when they have developed a strong inner mind. Lin-chi discussed this issue with his disciples to show them that they had the potential within to rise above difficulties:

> *Followers of the Way, this lone brightness before my*
> *eyes now, this person plainly listening to me—this*
> *person is unimpeded at any point but penetrates the*
> *ten directions, free to do as he pleases in the three-*
> *fold world. (Watson 1993, 33)*

Lin-chi's advice still holds true today. When you meet with adversity, whether in your own business or while working as part of a large company, the inner light of your own calm center can give you the strength of character to work well and succeed.

SHARING MEDITATION

In all relationships, keep the balance, maintain the Oneness. Seek to enhance Oneness. This goal is a criterion for peace and good relationships. Trust in the other and in yourself is essential. Trust is enhanced by meditating together.

You can share meditation. Frequently it is a group activity, with other seekers at Zen and Yoga centers, in daily meditation sessions or on meditation retreats. The master-student relationship is primary, but there are other relationships that are part of meditation. Some teach, some learn, some are guiding teachers signaling the changing rhythms of life—all perform social roles in groups of seekers, as monks. Yet meditation can also be shared in everyday life—and should be. Parents and children, couples, even business associates can meditate together. All who join in a meditation experience are less rife with interpersonal conflict.

GROUP MEDITATION EXERCISE

Bring together the people who wish to meditate. They may be people at work, your family, young or old. Sit down on the floor in a circle. Each person can find a comfortable seated position, usually cross-legged, although some might prefer to sit with their feet flat on the floor, knees bent. Be quiet and still, together. You might want to start with a two-minute session. Close your eyes if you like. All can allow their breathing to be natural and regular, and they should try to keep their shoulder muscles comfortably relaxed. If you choose to meditate together regularly, increase the time to at least ten minutes, sitting together in calm stillness. This can be a very nice experience to share. Other variations are possible, but the most important criterion is keep it simple, acceptable to all, and positive. The effects of sharing meditative experiences can be profound.

CONCLUSION

Meditation warms us and cools us, brings us calm while it soothes us, and helps us to face our lives with vitality and dignity. Maintain the mindful comfortableness of meditation as you meet the demands of life's circumstances. The innate wisdom of your deeper being is a resource to draw from, a wellspring for renewal and healing. This not only affects you but can also affect others around you who you care about.

The starting point, the center, must be your meditative experience. Finding your unique individual balance, you become able to influence your life to make it what you want it to be. Be willing to consider alternatives to your routines, new paths to follow. Learn to sense what is needed, and permit it. Pay attention to the various details of your life and take them seriously as they emerge. Follow the patterns and let the diverging views take form.

A larger orientation will gradually come to you, resolving things. It is already there in potential: the Oneness, unity, integrity. Oneness transcends circumstance—time, space, personal meaning, and problems. Be part of the Oneness and, from this perspective, many of life's problems will dissolve. The Way can guide you to what is fulfilling. You are inclined toward becoming complete: there is a tendency to seek balance, harmony of the center, homeostasis, which guides you subtly if you listen.

Enlightenment is not just a static practice. It is deep stillness that is intensely dynamic. This active life you lead is the source of your enlightenment, your path to living meditation.

> *We cannot conceive the formless form*
> *Of the space that we are seeing,*
> *Emptiness is the inner nature*
> *Within the outer form of being.*
> *We seek for unity, nevertheless*
> *To be at one is to be one*
> *With inconceivable peacefulness.*
> —C. Alexander Simpkins

BIBLIOGRAPHY

Adler, A. *Essays in Individual Psychology*. New York: Grove Press, 1959.

Allport, G. *Pattern and Growth in Personality*. New York: Holt, Rinehart and Winston, 1961.

American Translation, *A Barefoot Doctor's Manual*. Philadelphia: Running Press, 1977.

Atkinson, W. W. *Mind Power*. Chicago: Yoga Publication Society, 1912.

Beck, L. A. *The Story of Oriental Philosophy*. New York: New Home Library, 1928.

Bernard, C. *An Introduction to the Study of Experimental Medicine*. New York: Dover Publications, 1957.

Blofeld, J. *The Zen Teaching of Huang Po*. Boston: Shambhala, 1994.

Brooks, C. *Sensory Awareness: The Discovery of Experiencing*. Santa Barbara, Calif.: Ross Erikson Publishers, 1982.

Cannon, W. *The Wisdom of the Body*. New York: Norton, 1932.

Chall, J., and A. Mirsky. *Education and the Brain*. Chicago: University of Chicago Press, 1978.

Chan, W. T. *A Source Book in Chinese Philosophy*. Princeton, N.J.: Princeton University Press, 1963.

Cousins, N. *Anatomy of an Illness as Perceived by the Patient*. New York: Norton, 1979.

Dewey, J. *Democracy and Education*. New York: Macmillan, 1928.

Dohrenwend, B., and B. Dohrenwend. *Stressful Life Events and Their Concepts*. Brunswick, N.J.: Rutgers University Press, 1981.

Dumoulin, H. *Zen Buddhism: A History, India & China*. New York: Macmillan, 1988.

————. *Zen Buddhism: A History, Japan*. New York: Macmillan, 1990.

Dunlap, D. *Habits, Their Making and Unmaking*. New York: Liveright, 1932.

Duyvendak, J. J. L. *Tao te Ching*. Boston: Charles E. Tuttle Co., 1992.

Emerson, R. W. *Essays of Ralph Waldo Emerson.* New York: Thomas Y. Crowell Co., 1926.

Evans-Wentz, W. Y. *Tibetan Yoga and Secret Doctrines.* New York: Oxford University Press, 1935.

Gazzaniga, M., and J. LeDoux. *The Integrated Mind.* New York: Plenum Press, 1978.

Gelhorn, E., and W. Kiely. "Mystical States of Consciousness: Neurophysiological and Clinical Aspects." *Biofeedback and Self Control.* Chicago: Aldine Publishing Co., 1973.

Herrigel, E. *Zen in the Art of Archery.* New York: Vintage Books, 1953.

Herrigel, G. *Zen in the Art of Flower Arrangement.* London: Arkana, 1958.

Hinkle, L. "The Concept of Stress in Biological and Social Sciences." Lipowski, Z. J., et al., eds. *Psychosomatic Medicine.* New York: Oxford University Press, 1977.

Insko, C. A. *Theories of Attitude Change.* New York: Appleton-Century-Crofts, 1967.

James, W. *Selected Papers on Philosophy by William James.* London: J. M. Dent & Sons, 1918.

————. *Pragmatism and the Meaning of Truth.* Cambridge: Harvard University Press, 1978.

————. *Principles of Psychology.* 2 vols. New York: Henry Holt and Company, 1896.

Janet, P. *Psychological Healing,* 2 vols. London: George Allen Unwin Ltd., 1925.

Janis, I. *Stress and Frustration.* New York: Harcourt Brace Jovanovich, 1971.

Keene, B. *Sensing, Letting Yourself Live.* San Francisco: Harper & Row, 1979.

Konvitz, M. R., and G. Kennedy. *The American Pragmatists.* New York: The World Publishing Co., 1969.

Lazarus, R. "Psychological Stress and Coping in Adaptation and Illness." Lipowski, Z. J., et al., eds. *Psychosomatic Medicine.* New York: Oxford University Press, 1977.

Legge, J. *The Texts of Taoism,* 2 vols. New York: Dover, 1962.

Loori, J. D. "The Sacredness of Work." Whitmyer, C., ed. *Mindfulness & Meaningful Work.* Berkeley, Calif.: Parallax Press, 1994.

Matarazzo, J. *Wechsler's Measurement and Appraisal of Adult Intelligence.* Baltimore: Williams and Wilkins Co., 1972.

Merton, T. *Zen and the Birds of Appetite,* New York: New Directions, 1968.

Oyama, M. *The Kyokushin Way.* Tokyo: Japan Publications, 1979.

Pine, R. *The Zen Teaching of Bodhidharma.* San Francisco: North Point Press, 1989.

Price, A.F., and W. Mou-lam. *The Diamond Sutra and the Sutra of Hui-Neng*. Boston: Shambhala, 1990.

Rapaport, D. *Emotions and Memory*. New York: International University Press, 1971.

Reps, P. *Zen Flesh, Zen Bones*. Rutland, Vt.: Charles E. Tuttle Co., 1980

Roach, M. "Meditation's Magic." *Health Magazine*. America Online, 1995.

Rossi, E. *The Psychobiology of Mind-Body Healing*. New York: Norton, 1986.

_____., ed. *The Collected Papers of Milton H. Erickson*. New York: Irvington, 1980.

Samuels, M., and N. Samuels, *Seeing with the Mind's Eye*. New York: Random House, 1975.

Selye, H. *Stress Without Distress*. New York: Signet, 1974.

_____. *The Stress of Life*, New York: McGraw Hill, 1976.

Seung Sahn, *The Whole World Is a Single Flower*. Boston: Charles E. Tuttle Co., 1992.

Simonton, C. O. *Getting Well Again*. Los Angeles: Tarcher, 1978.

Simpkins, C.A., and A. M. Simpkins. *Principles of Meditation*. Boston: Charles E. Tuttle Co., 1996.

_____. *Principles of Self Hypnosis*. New York: Irvington, 1993.

_____. *Zen Around the World*. Boston: Charles E. Tuttle Co., 1997.

Suzuki, D. T. *The Training of the Zen Buddhist Monk*. Boston: Charles E. Tuttle Co., 1994.

_____. *The Zen Doctrine of No Mind*. York, Maine: Samuel Weiser, 1969.

_____. *Zen and Japanese Culture*. Princeton, N.J.: Princeton University Press, 1959.

Taylor, L. *A Woman's Book of Yoga*. Boston: Charles E. Tuttle Co., 1993.

Wachter, S. "Special Report: Zen and the Art of Japanese Health." American On-line, May 12, 1994.

Waddell, N. *The Unborn*. San Francisco: North Point Press, 1984.

Watson, B. *The Zen Teachings of Master Lin-Chi*. Boston: Shambhala, 1993.

Watts, A. *The Way of Zen*. New York: Vintage Books, 1957.

Whitehorn, J. C. "The Healthful Benefits of Stress." *Journal of Chronic Diseases* 4, no. 6 (December 1956).

Whitmyer, C. *Mindfulness and Meaningful Work*. Berkeley, Calif.: Parallax Press, 1994.

Williams, G. "Hopping-Heart Stopping Mad." *Longevity*, August 15, 1994.

Yutang, L. *The Wisdom of China and India*. New York: Random House, 1952.

Zimmer, J. "New Credo for Fitness." *New York Times*, March 27, 1996.